British Re   nd Development Aircraft 1945–65

Volume 1

CRAIG VAUGHTON

KEY
Books

Front cover image: Hawker P.1081, built from the second P.1052 development aircraft VX279, the next step after the Sea Hawk, with swept wings and tail. The genesis of the Hunter that followed is clearly visible.

Title page image: Avro 707C, WZ744, the only two seater built of five development aircraft for the Vulcan.

Contents page image: Developed during Word War Two, the versatile Meteor soldiered on in RAF service. NF.14 WS739, now at Newark Air Museum, was eventually replaced in 1956 by the Gloster Javelin.

Back cover image: Hawker Hunter T.7 two-seat trainer at Newark Air Museum. Progressive improvements over the life of the Hunter reaped rewards for Hawker.

Dedication
Dedicated to the brave souls who helped push the boundaries of powered flight but flew too close to the sun.

Acknowledgements
Many thanks to my friend Babs Whelan for taking time out of her wedding cake business to photograph the Short SC.1 at Ulster Folk and Transport Museum in Northern Ireland. Should anyone need wedding cakes in that part of the world, please head to www.wedcakes.co.uk

Thanks also go to my fellow former RAF colleagues, John Nicholls for stopping me falling asleep while driving back from yet another trip for more photographs, and Andrew Paine for sanity checking my ramblings!

Naturally, to my family, for the encouragement to finish the project and just letting me get on with it, especially through a tough first half of 2023: this is for you, mum.

All the photos of the models seen here were taken at the RAF Museum Midlands.

Published by Key Books
An imprint of Key Publishing Ltd
PO Box 100
Stamford
Lincs PE9 1XQ

www.keypublishing.com

Copyright © Craig Vaughton, 2024

ISBN 978 1 80282 642 5

Typeset by SJmagic DESIGN SERVICES, India.

Contents

Introduction

By the end of World War Two, the British aircraft industry was on a high, especially after bringing the Gloster Meteor jet fighter into service, an aircraft capable of matching any other in the world. However, the technical intelligence that returned from Germany following the Fedden Mission – an explorative mission to investigate German technology, including aircraft and aeroengines – came as a shock to both the government and industry. The mission highlighted that in terms of aircraft design and research, along with the facilities to enable it, Britain was far behind. With a government focussed on getting the country back on its feet, funding constraints meant manufacturers largely had to invest their own funds into jet engine technology research and the airframes needed to support it.

With a preoccupied government, military chiefs who moved the requirement goalposts too frequently and a shortage of skilled labour, one might expect the post-war aviation industry to have contracted and then consolidated. Strange as it seems, however, the aircraft manufacturers scattered across the British Isles managed, for close to two decades, to produce flying wonders that captivated the nation. Test pilots displayed these winged marvels at air shows such as Farnborough and were hailed as heroes. Their appearances were immortalised in black and white by Pathé newsreels in the cinema or shown on the BBC news, as well as recorded in the press and avidly followed by many a short-trousered boy.

This 'golden age' in aircraft evolution was brought about by the many technological advances of the war and the need to explore flight envelopes, control systems and airframe designs of those years. Even before the end of hostilities in Europe and the Far East, and certainly once the tide of war had turned in favour of the Allies, individuals, and later in Britain, at least, government-appointed committees had started to consider the post-war world of aviation for both military and civil purposes. In World War One, the fragile biplanes of 1914 had given way to sturdier, faster, machine gun-armed fighters and multi-engine bombers of 1918. Similarly, the six years of hostilities between 1939 and 1945 had distilled the development process of aircraft, engines and the equipment fitted to them. High-performance piston engines had been joined by the first gas turbine, jet-engine fighters on a few front-line squadrons in both Germany and England before hostilities ceased. In addition to the Me 262, the Luftwaffe also had, by 1944, the rocket-engine Me 163 (Komet) fighter operational, with a whole raft of aircraft designs either on drawing boards or part finished, many bordering on sheer genius. All of these were avidly exploited by other designers in the Soviet Union and the West.

Aircraft were eventually equipped with air-intercept and surface-search radars, air-to-surface guided missiles and ultimately, for a short time, one country alone possessed the ability to deliver a single bomb capable of destroying a city. All these developments had begun to shape the vision for future military aircraft, as well as that of their designers. While the application of the jet engine to civilian aircraft lagged behind its military counterparts, it's here where the majority of the population would eventually experience the benefits of those leaps in aircraft performance. The post-war civilian aviation industry also saw de Haviland's fortunes unexpectedly dashed by building the world's first jet-powered airliner, the DH.106 Comet, only to encounter the impact of stress fatigue in metals. The delays in curing these problems allowed the US manufacturers time to release their first civil jet liners. However, this setback meant the market was open for American companies to rule the civilian skies until Europe's Airbus began to challenge the manufacturers of that nation more than 20 years later. Often though, civilian aircraft builders regularly had their plans derailed by the British airlines themselves, rather than by competitors overseas.

The Hawker Sea Fury, Avro Lincoln and Bristol Brabazon possibly represented the zenith of piston-powered fighter, bomber and passenger aircraft development in Britain. Yet, the arrival of the jet engine quickly rendered most of the propeller-driven aircraft that had gone before obsolete. In order to take advantage of the jet engine and the potential it undoubtedly offered, a great deal of experimentation was needed to ensure that the replacement for the last generation of piston-driven aircraft would not just get off the ground, by actually perform as expected, and return safely. In a world before computers could model virtually anything, the only way to achieve this was developmental aircraft. This could be in the form of flying scale models or full-size test aircraft. Often these development aircraft were built purely to explore one or more particular part of the flight envelope: new wing shapes such as the delta wing, mixed jet and rocket power, or even a designer's brainwave!

Aircraft development continued until government white papers, project cancellations and forced company mergers reduced the famous brand names in aircraft design to a shadow of their former selves, with manufacturers only willing to build aircraft for contracts the government had placed.

This book documents the surviving aircraft from that golden age; these are the remaining research and development machines that contributed to the bank of knowledge needed to push forward aircraft evolution. It broaches on Britain's requirement to build its own atomic weapon and the impact of that weapon on the design of the aircraft intended to carry it. Alongside the development-only aircraft, there are the prototypes and pre-production aircraft that have to be built in order to get a machine safely into operational service with the British and other armed forces. Context is provided with a review of the decisions made by governments of assorted persuasions, or the armed forces, which often axed projects or simply changed their minds.

The final version of the subsonic Gloster Javelin to see service was the FAW.9R. XH892, seen here at the Norfolk and Suffolk Aviation Museum. A more advanced supersonic thin wing version was cancelled in 1956, before the Javelin had fully entered Royal Air Force (RAF) service.

Chapter 1

A Tangled Web – Companies, White Papers and Cancellations

At first sight, through the 1930s and into the 1950s, Great Britain appeared to have numerous separate aircraft manufacturers scattered across the country. Avro, Hawker and Supermarine were household names, especially during the war years. However, less apparent was how intertwined the aircraft companies actually were, and for how long they had been so.

Hawker and Avro along with Gloster were, in fact, all part of the Hawker Siddeley group and had been since 1935. However, each named company ran its own independent design departments, all with numerous draftsmen and engineers as well as administrative staff. Hence, when the Air Ministry or civil airlines were looking for new machines, each entity essentially competed against the other. This plethora of design departments and manufacturing facilities was acceptable during the years of relatively slow technological progress between the wars. During World War Two, the dispersed nature of the manufacturing sites was a huge bonus, but once the conflict ended, it was considered inefficient. With the great cost involved in building and testing prototypes and a financially crippled post-war economy, it became obvious to those in the industry that there were simply too many companies competing for contracts from a government short of funds, not to mention a lack of skilled labour and material resources.

The initial lethargic rate of aircraft development was largely due to British government thinking that suggested that, following the end of World War Two, the country was unlikely to fight another major war for at least ten years. Ministers in Whitehall therefore considered there was time to develop new technologies before needing them to be deployed. The outbreak of the Korean War in 1950 soon crushed that theory, especially when swept-wing Russian MiG 15s appeared, powered by an unlicensed derivative of a Rolls-Royce Nene engine given to the Soviets by the post-war Labour government. The Soviets had simply reverse engineered it, eventually producing the Klimov VK-1. (Rolls-Royce receiving not one rouble in return.) This was at a time when the Royal Navy carriers deployed to Korea were still fielding piston-powered Sea Furies, Seafires and Fireflies, while the Commonwealth forces were equipped with Mustangs and Meteors.

By the early 1950s, in an effort to resolve the delays getting newer British aircraft into service, the government issued 'super priority' notices to ensure the manufacturers of certain aircraft, including the Hunter and Swift, then under development, were supplied with adequate materials and manpower. However, this did not stop the Royal Air Force (RAF) having to equip 11 squadrons with American Sabre's between 1953 and 1956. There were potential British options in place of the Sabre, such as the Hawker P.1081 or Supermarine Type 535 that with a little development could have filled this gap, but it was still quicker and ultimately cheaper to employ the Sabre. Another problem was that so many super priority contracts were issued, not just for aircraft, that everybody struggled to differentiate what was

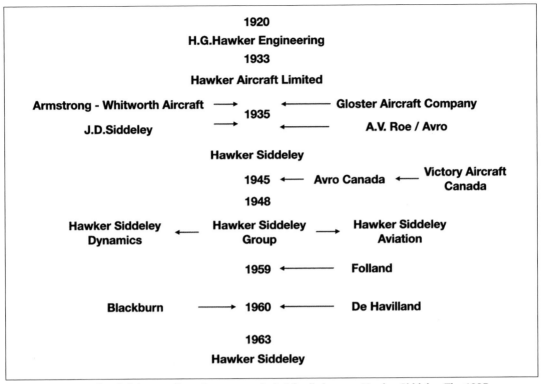

What's in a name? The slightly complicated structure of what finally became Hawker Siddeley. The 1935 acquisition of Armstrong Whitworth Aircraft seems quite strange, as the remainder of Armstrong Whitworth Engineering became part of Vickers at the same time.

Engine manufacturers merged following the government's rationalisation policy. Rolls-Royce bought out Bristol Siddeley in 1966, before financial problems in the early 1970s were the catalyst for its own restructuring.

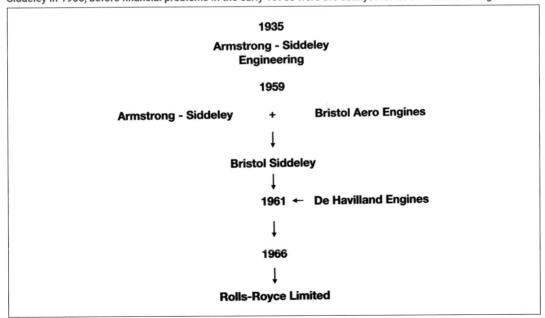

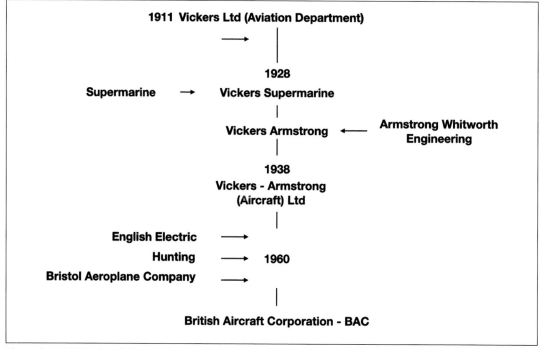

1911 Vickers Ltd (Aviation Department)

1928

Supermarine   →   **Vickers Supermarine**

Vickers Armstrong   ←   **Armstrong Whitworth Engineering**

1938
Vickers - Armstrong (Aircraft) Ltd

English Electric   →

Hunting   →   **1960**

Bristol Aeroplane Company   →

British Aircraft Corporation - BAC

The path to British Aircraft Corporation (BAC): Less convoluted than Hawker Siddeley, with the 1960 inclusion of English Electric, Hunting and Bristol's aircraft business a result of mandated rationalisation. Vickers and its chairman George Edwards would wield considerable influence in government circles during much of the 1950s and '60s.

actually a priority and what was not. In addition, the these contracts did nothing to boost the availability of materials or skilled labour to industry.

Eventually, the British government opted to rationalise the industry, and it used the biggest stick it had to coerce the companies into mergers: contracts for new aircraft. Simultaneously, some in government believed that the missile alone could replace fighter and bomber aircraft, and this thinking had a significant long-term impact on British aviation.

Missing from the companies that were forced to merge, but whose aircraft appear later, is Short Brothers, which, after being nationalised in 1943, had by 1947 closed all its wartime UK mainland factories, leaving all remaining production concentrated in Belfast by 1948. As a major employer for the province, the British government largely left it alone, as it did with manufacturer Scottish Aviation for similar reasons.

Fulcrum: The 1957 Defence White Paper

Dated 15 March 1957 and announced in the House of Commons by then-defence minister Duncan Sandys, the Defence White Paper (DWP) has come to be regarded as the single most damaging act of government to the aircraft industry in the UK. That it had a far more wide-ranging impact is usually forgotten, Government thinking was affected by the US reaction to the Anglo-French invasion of the Suez Canal zone in 1956. But much of its decision making was a response to the inadequacies in equipment and force availability that this operation highlighted, resulting in a major reorganisation of military structures and requirements. In what also becomes a common refrain in the following years, it addressed the financial impact of paying for defence, slimming the defence budget again. Foremost, it heralded the winding down of national service after 1960 and, as a result, reduced and reorganised the size of the British Army, which previously had been the largest recipient of recruits. UK Armed forces personnel was to be reduced by 65,000 within one year, falling to 375,000 by 1962[1]. It also scrapped the Air Branch of the Royal Navy Volunteer Reserve (RNVR), which followed the previous curtailing of its operations in 1947. The document paved the way for the rationalisation of the industries supporting military procurement, not just in aviation, but it was undoubtedly the aircraft industry that felt the biggest long-term impact and the reason for which the white paper is remembered.

The DWP cancelled virtually all manned military aircraft projects, certainly those where 'the roles previously carried out by aircraft could henceforth be carried out using missiles'. One exception for the RAF was the English Electric Lightning, deemed to be in such an advanced state of development that it would be allowed to continue and enter service, nominally to fill the gap before the defensive missile systems arrived. The other was still a paper plane, the early designs for General Operation Requirement 339, what would in time become TSR.2. Inexplicably though, despite this emphasis on rocketry, a number of existing missile projects were also cancelled.

The number of aircraft companies was also to be reduced, with the numerous smaller companies reorganised into fewer, larger ones. In order to achieve this, future major government aircraft contracts were to be issued for the aircraft being built with additional clauses that in essence obliged the contracted agency to merge with the other companies involved in the build. This was a government-enforced rationalisation, with the implied threat that until companies agreed to the government's demands, no further work would come their way. Refusal to merge precluded any government contracts being directly handed out to Handley Page after the Victor bomber project was completed and ultimately led to the company's demise in 1970.[2]

The result reduced the number of separate aircraft production and design companies to three major conglomerates: the British Aircraft Corporation (BAC) and Hawker Siddeley Aviation (HSA) as the fixed-wing aircraft producers, and Westland Helicopters as builders of all rotorcraft.

The aero engine companies were not immune to this slimming down process either. Armstrong Siddeley merged with Bristol Aero Engines to become Bristol Siddeley and soon after also absorbed the engine division of de Havilland. Seemingly aloof from all this was Rolls-Royce, whose introduction into the jet engine business was surprisingly courtesy of Rover cars, which exchanged its wartime jet engine production factory at Barnoldswick, for the Rolls-Royce Meteor tank engine business. This handed over what were, for the most part, originally Frank Whittle's designs that Rover factories had been producing. Of these designs, one went on to become the Rolls-Royce Welland, and another became the Derwent.

Rolls-Royce later went on to take over Napier engines in 1961, which was part of English Electric, whose gas turbine engines were powering the Westland Wessex helicopter by this time, as well as the Eland fitted to the Fairey Rotodyne. By 1966, Rolls-Royce acquired Bristol Siddeley, leaving it as the sole large-scale UK aero engine manufacturer.

Projects Cancelled Under the 1957 Defence White Paper

Avro 730: Designed to meet the 1954 Specification R.156T and Operational Requirement (OR) 330 for a supersonic high-altitude reconnaissance aircraft, which later evolved to include strategic nuclear and conventional bombing capability. The Bristol 188, which was in essence a scale model of the Avro 730 and built to explore kinetic heating at high speed that the 730 was expected to encounter, didn't fly until 1962, and by 1957 the Air Ministry finally accepted that the increased effectiveness of Soviet surface-to-air missiles (SAMs) and supersonic fighters would require a switch to low-level attack for which the 730 was unsuited. Consequently, the ministry had already advised the government to cancel Avro 730 ahead of its official cancellation in the DWP.

---

1   Ministry of Defence, 'Defence: Outline of Future Policy', HMSO, 1957.
2   The HP.115 research aircraft for the Concorde programme was subcontracted by BAC to Handley Page.

The futuristic-looking Avro 730, with wing-mounted engine pods, each housing four Armstrong Siddeley P.176 turbo jets.

SR.177 was considerably larger than the SR.53, but a vastly more capable proposition.

Saunders Roe SR.P177: This was a larger and fully equipped aircraft based on a similar mixed power jet engine and rocket technology derived from the winning designs submitted for Specification F.124T of 1952, which had resulted in the SR.53. The P.177R was cancelled for the RAF as a direct result of the DWP; the P.177N for the Royal Navy survived until August 1957 after some political infighting in Westminster. There were still hopes of sales to West Germany though, with the help of NATO funding, which was unexpectedly refused after German interest switched to the Lockheed F-104. The reasons behind this refusal only surfaced years after the event, when Lockheed was fined for bribing numerous influential people involved in aircraft contracts that ensured the F-104 won huge orders worldwide.

Fairey Long Range Interceptor: This was the winning submission for an advanced, long-range, all-weather interceptor required by the 1955 Specification F.155T. The Armstrong Whitworth AW.169 was selected as a 'back up'. Unofficially known as the Delta 3 or Delta Large, this was a considerably scaled-up development of the Fairey Delta 2, even retaining the droop snoot nose. It was powered by two

'Fairey Large' was designed to specification F.155T and more than double the size of the Fairey Delta 2; should development of this aircraft have continued, advances in technology may have made it obsolete before it arrived in service.

A finished P.1121 would have looked similar to this model of P.1103, but without the wing sponsons and with a single seat cockpit. P.1103 was Hawker's submission for F.155T.

Rolls-Royce RB.133 engines, plus a pair of de Havilland Spectre Junior rocket motors and was destined to be armed with a Vickers Red Dean air-to-air missile under each wing. With an estimated all-up-weight of more than 50,000lb, this would be a big aircraft for a fighter, akin to the Soviet Tu-28 'Fiddler' in size, though much quicker, but both British and Soviet aircraft were designed as bomber destroyers as opposed to engaging in dogfights with other fighters.

The P.1121 mock-up at Kingston. Prototype production was not this advanced, and what remains of it is a nose section and forward fuselage that still exist. The RAF Museum have been trying to find a suitable home for these since 2021.

Hawker P.1121: Not strictly cancelled by the 1957 DWP, because no requirement or orders for it ever existed, but the DWP effectively blocked any potential interest in it, and despite further limited funding by Hawker, the project folded in 1958. Derived from Hawker's failed submission for Specification F.115T, the P.1103, which the Air Ministry had decided was too small, Hawker persevered with the general airframe design and developing it as a private venture, to become the P.1121. Powered by a single de Havilland Gyron engine, and armed with a pair of air-to-air missiles and two Aden cannon, it had an anticipated top speed of Mach 2.35 at altitude and Mach 1.35 at sea level. It's highly plausible that, given Hawker's track record, P.1121 could have fulfilled a multi-role fighter mission much the same as the RAF's F4M Phantom eventually undertook more than ten years later.

Short Seamew: The forgotten aircraft of the 1957 carnage, the Seamew was already in production, with 24 having flown and several had been accepted by the Royal Navy. However, few tears were shed at its demise, with the prototype having what were described as 'vicious handling qualities'. Despite numerous modifications prior to production, it was never wholly satisfactory. Powered by a single Armstrong Siddeley Mamba turboprop, it had a strange humped forward fuselage and a long, fixed undercarriage. It was designed predominantly for land-based operations from hastily prepared airstrips with RAF Coastal Command. It also had the ability to operate without the need for catapult launch from any Royal Navy aircraft carrier. It was

A flight of 4 Short Seamew AS.1. A total of 26 were built, but all were scrapped.

scheduled to be manned by Royal Naval Volunteer Reserve (RNVR) aircrew. The Seamew was conceived as suitable for mass production in an effort to counter the growing numbers of Soviet submarines. The variant intended for RAF use had already been cancelled in 1956, but the 1957 DWP cancelled the remaining order for the Royal Navy, and also consigned those already delivered to the breaker's yard.

If anything, the Seamew was an aircraft that should never have been commissioned, specifically since orders for the much larger and more capable Gannet had already been placed and at a time when the versatility and utility of the helicopter were becoming readily apparent, in that every surface vessel in the Royal Navy that was able to operate the Westland Wasp (which first appeared in 1958) became a viable anti-submarine platform.

Covered in a later chapter, but also lost to the same white paper was Blue Envoy, a highly advanced ramjet-powered SAM, on a par with the CIM-10 Bombarc. The Bombarc was operated by the United States Air Force and Royal Canadian Air Force until the 1970s.

As for missiles in place of aircraft, more than 60 years later and the UK still does not possess, and has never possessed, a missile defence system with nationwide coverage. In addition, until the first Polaris-equipped nuclear submarines entered operational service in 1968 with the Royal Navy, the country did not have any form of offensive strategic missile capability.

Following the 1957 DWP, it took three years for sanity to prevail and full development of manned combat aircraft resumed, but five aircraft, along with two engine projects had already been scrapped. If Britain was to have any sort of lead in aviation development, this one act of government intervention did absolutely nothing to aid it.

Chapter 2
Boulton Paul P111

The need to explore new wing designs as well as the ways in which minor changes impacted overall aircraft handling were constant themes revisited with many research aircraft, from the immediate post-war period and into the late 1960s. The Boulton Paul P111 was one such aircraft: produced to Specification E.27/47, which called for an aircraft to gain insight into delta wing shapes and the handling of aircraft that used them at transonic speeds. What appeared was essentially the smallest airframe that could be built to house a Rolls-Royce Nene jet engine. It combined a thin delta wing with the ability to have a set of different wing-tip profiles, facilitated via three sets of bolt-on glass-reinforced plastic (GRP) extensions. Strangely, despite having this adaptability, the aircraft flew most of the time in a full delta configuration and with pointed wing tips. The centrifugal flow Nene engine resulted in a somewhat tubby-looking fuselage, while the oval-shaped nose air intake resembled a set of pursed lips. The tall nose wheel leg gave the aircraft a nose-up attitude on the ground, but this was needed to place the wing at the correct angle of attack for optimum airflow on take-off and landing.

First flown on 10 October 1950 by Sqn Ldr Bob Smyth, the P111 was found to be a sensitive aircraft to fly, especially on take-off, and much of this was down to the powered controls. Previously, the pilot

'Yellow Peril'; Boulton Paul P.111A. (Midland Air Museum)

could feel the effect of control movements as the ailerons and elevators were connected by cables and pulleys to the control column. The effort needed to move them therefore changed according to airspeed and consequently air pressure exerted on them. However, there was no such feedback from the new hydraulically powered controls. To remedy this, the pilot's controls were revised and spring-loaded after a few months to offer some semblance of feedback.

A belly-up landing when the undercarriage failed to deploy could have terminated the research programme for good, but after a meeting between Boulton Paul, the Royal Aircraft Establishment (RAE) and one of the test pilots, Jock Elliot, the aircraft went back to Boulton Paul for the incorporation of variable gearing between the control column and the flying controls. This style of mechanism had existed for some time, including fitment in Schneider Trophy designs of the inter-war period and it eventually evolved into what is usually called 'Q-feel'. While the aircraft was at Boulton Paul, engineers also addressed some of the other issues highlighted by the flying programme; consequently four petal-shaped air brakes were added to the fuselage; and the undercarriage doors were redesigned to reduce the large trim change induced when they retracted or deployed. The nose intake for the engine also benefited from a redesign to improve airflow, while a long pitot tube was fitted in the centre partition of the air intake to improve the air pressure feed for cockpit instrumentation.

The aircraft re-emerged in July 1953 as the P111A for further flight trials, resplendent in a bright yellow finish in place of the previous natural metal. Needless to say, it wasn't long before it gained the nickname 'the Yellow Peril'. Over time, modifications continued to be made, including strengthening the anti-spin parachute to allow its deployment as a brake parachute to shorten the landing run.

The P111A flew from Boscombe Down for a further five years until 1958 when it was transferred to the Cranfield College of Aeronautics as a training airframe. In 1975, it was acquired by the Midland Aircraft Preservation Society and transferred to the Midland Air Museum.

In 1952, Boulton Paul built one more development aircraft, the P120. This was very similar in shape and size to the P111 but incorporated a swept fin and rudder with high-mounted tail surfaces and

Bolton Paul P.111A; note the long-nose leg to give the wings the optimum take-off angle. This became a feature on many delta-wing jets. (Midland Air Museum)

was designed to investigate these features in conjunction with a delta wing. Deemed to have far more pleasant flying characteristics than the P111, the P120 was readied for the Farnborough Airshow in September 1952, complete with a stunning gloss black paint scheme, but crashed on 28 August in an accident attributed to excessive flutter causing the loss of the port elevator. Fortunately, test pilot 'Ben' Gunn ejected to safety and in doing so became the first pilot to eject from a delta-winged aircraft.

After proposing but finding no takers for a number of vertical take-off aircraft designs following the P120, Boulton Paul finally withdrew from aircraft manufacture, but the company's development of powered flying controls continued and the systems first incorporated in the P111A were developed further, finally finding their way into Concorde and other aircraft. Boulton Paul was bought by Dowty Ltd in 1961 to become Dowty Boulton Paul and then Dowty Aerospace. Now part of Smith Industries Group, Dowty remains one of the world's major names in aircraft control systems.

Above: The sharp-pointed fin was never really seen again on any other delta-winged aircraft. The side view underlines the diminutive size of the aircraft.

Left: VT935 sits in the shadow of a rather more familiar delta in the shape of XL360, Midland Air Museum's Avro Vulcan B2.

P.111 in its original guise, with a smaller, more rounded nose intake and in a natural metal finish. The black cheatline extends from the anti-dazzle panel ahead of the cockpit, rather than from the intake seen in the P.111A.

P.111A head on.

The short-lived follow-on to the P.111, the P.120 introduced swept-tail surfaces and much improved handling compared to the P.111.

Chapter 3

Flying Prone

The Reid and Sigrist R&S Bobsleigh, now at Newark Air Museum.

In terms of creating an aircraft purely for research, the Reid and Sigrist (R&S) Desford/Bobsleigh and the Prone Meteor were definitely trips down a very strange road.

It had long been understood that the physical stresses exerted on a pilot, especially during combat manoeuvres, had led to a number of aircraft losses and pilot fatalities.[3] The adoption of dedicated aircraft for dive-bombing in the inter-war years was one area where the repercussions of the pilot losing consciousness were catastrophic. The Luftwaffe even installed a limited-function auto-pilot in the Ju-87 Stuka, which automatically engaged to control the aircraft as it came out of what might otherwise have been a terminal bomb run.

Prone Meteor

During the early 1950s, rapid increases in aircraft speeds following the adoption of jet power meant that the RAF started looking again into the effects of high G-forces and the idea of a pilot flying in a prone position, both of which resulted in the Prone Meteor. The final Meteor F8 off the production line, WK935, was built with a nose extension housing a second cockpit for a semi-prone pilot, complete with a special couch seat and a custom set of controls.

---

3 The symptoms, eventually termed 'grey outs', caused by positive G-forces, and 'red outs', caused by negative G, had all been reported by those fortunate enough to have survived.

The Prone Meteor F8 at RAF Museum Midlands. Access to the front cockpit was via a hatch inside the nose wheel bay. Emergency egress would have been less than rapid.

A close up view of the nose of the Prone Meteor F8. Despite the bubble canopy, it's hardly surprising that all-round vision was difficult, considering the pilot would be lying almost face down.

Although 55 hours of flying were carried out, the results essentially showed that although flying from a prone position was feasible, it offered no major advantage over a conventional seat, while at the same time, greatly reducing the rearward vision for the pilot. The invention of G-suits for pilots was found to be much easier to implement: a G-force-sensitive valve controls the pressure, which is applied via a series of inflation tubes that constrict the lower torso and legs, thus preventing the flow of blood away from the main torso and brain during high-G manoeuvres and delaying the onset of a black out.

With modern aircraft able to sustain G-forces on their structures that are considerably greater than those a pilot can generally sustain (around 9G), it leaves the human as the weakest component in the air battle. The appearance of drones, such as Boeing's Loyal Wingman and British Aerospace (BAe) describing its Tempest stealth fighter as capable of being manned or unmanned, begs the question of how long the weakest link will remain in the air as an active participant, rather than being left on the ground with the remote control.

WK935 was retired in 1957 and now resides at the RAF Museum Midlands at RAF Cosford.

Reid and Sigrist Desford/Bobsleigh

At the same time as research was being carried out into high speeds, the impact of flying prone at low speeds was also being investigated.

Originally built as a trainer just as the war ended, the R&S R.S.3 Desford was an attractive two-seat, low-wing monoplane powered by a pair of de Havilland Gipsy Major engines. With the war over and the consequent glut of surplus aircraft, R&S found no takers for its new machine within the British armed forces, though by May 1949, it was flying as VZ728 with RAF markings.

The RS.3 Desford as it originally looked. The RAF roundel and P for prototype markings ahead of the G-AGOS registration are just visible.

The R&S Desford after nasal surgery. With a good forward view and side windows, it's easy to see why it was later used for aerial photography.

With no other use for it, the Desford underwent major surgery and reappeared as the R.S.4 Bobsleigh in June 1951 to carry out low-speed prone pilot trials. As with the Meteor, a new longer front fuselage was installed, with a glazed nose and in this case, side windows to aid all-round visibility. Also, like the Meteor, the results of the test flying were inconclusive, though once completed, unlike the Meteor, the R.S.4 returned to the civilian register and was used until the early 1970s as an air photography platform by Film Aviation Services.

Restored to flying condition in 2018, the R.S.4 found a permanent home at Newark Air Museum in August 2022.

Chapter 4

Civil Affairs and the Avro Ashton

In among the rocket-engine fighters and delta wings, the Avro 760 Ashton II is one of few surviving prototypes with any sort of link to the civilian airliners produced during the immediate post-war period. Of the jet-engine passenger aircraft built during the period, there are few surviving original prototypes. The first BAC 1-11 prototype (G-ASHG) crashed; those for Trident (G-ARPA) and VC10 (G-ARTA) were broken up in the 1970s. The Comet (G-ALVG) met a similar fate in the 1950s, although the Comet 4C prototype (G-AOVU) does survive at the Seattle Museum of Flight in the USA. There are no complete surviving prototypes in the UK of any of the large propeller-driven types either; the nose of the second Britannia prototype, G-ALRX, being about the largest section and this came after extraction from the muddy banks of the River Severn following a crash in 1953. Even the much smaller prototype Scottish Aviation Twin Pioneer crashed in 1960.

Many of the immediate post-war civilian aircraft designs were conceived as a result of the Brabazon Committee. Established by the British government in 1942, it was tasked to explore the requirements for the civilian aircraft market in the British Empire and beyond once hostilities had ceased. Some of the reasoning behind its formation became rather prophetic. When the war began, civilian transport aircraft production and development stopped, with all production switched to bombers and fighters, while any transport aircraft needed would be sourced from the USA. What was readily apparent as a result of this decision, is that it would leave the field open after the war for the USA to dominate the civilian airliner market, as Britain would have had little to offer. Some in government also appreciated that the numbers employed in aircraft production when the switch from war to peace occurred would drop dramatically and efforts should be made to preserve especially the skilled jobs, let alone a civilian aircraft industry. Having something to offer a reborn commercial aircraft market would also see the country benefit from export sales and the prestige of selling British technology abroad.

Brabazon Committee recommendations can be split into two sections. In an attempt to get a head start on producing civilian models, it was recommended that four interim types be built, based on adapting existing bomber and flying boat designs. Success here was very mixed, having to compete against established and generally better American models, especially the likes of the Lockheed Constellation and Douglas DC-6, though all the interim types saw extensive use during the Berlin Airlift of 1948.

The Interim 'Adaption' Bomber-Derived Aircraft

- Avro York – converted from the Lancaster and already in service in limited numbers by 1945. British Overseas Airways Corporation (BOAC) operated 25 passenger Yorks until the early 1950s, mainly to Europe and South Africa.
- Avro Tudor – converted from the Lincoln bomber, itself derived from the earlier Lancaster. Seen as stop-gap for the transatlantic route pending arrival of the Brabazon Type 1, with a Mk2 filling in before arrival of the aircraft built to meet the Type 3 specification (see below). Plagued with reliability problems, poor handling and slow development, it was also unpopular because of the tail wheel undercarriage.

- Handley Page Hermes – derived from the Halifax III, development delays eventually saw it adopted in 1950 by BOAC when the Mk4 arrived. Unlike the other interim land planes, it at least had a tricycle undercarriage.
- Short Sandringham – converted from the Sunderland flying boat. Seven different versions were built, with the unique nature of the flying boat seeing some still in operation until the 1970s.

The suggested new types were to be built to compete on the transatlantic routes, replace pre-war types on the lengthy 'Empire' routes and the multitude of smaller types found on shorter European routes, (including the popular but outdated DH.89 Rapide biplane), as well as try to take over from large numbers of war surplus types, especially the ubiquitous Douglas DC-3. What is noticeable though, is all were still propeller driven and not until the Type 4 was included at the insistence of Sir Geoffrey de Havilland, who as chairman of de Havilland aircraft and engine companies, knew what the company had on the drawing boards, was a turbojet-powered aircraft involved.

The New Types

- Type 1 – A very large, long-range aircraft, optimsed for transatlantic routes, this resulted in the Bristol Brabazon.
- Type 2A – A replacement for the DC-3/C-47 Dakota, still piston engined, which led to the Airspeed Ambassador.
- Type 2B – A replacement for the DC-3/C-47 Dakota, powered by turboprop engines, with the Vickers Viscount leading the way.
- Type 3 – A large-four-engine, medium-range landplane for the Empire routes, which after much evolution eventually resulted in the Bristol Britannia.
- Type 4 – A jet-propelled, high-speed, 100-seater, though initially envisaged as a high-speed mail carrier, a specification written especially for the DH Comet.
- Type 5A – A twin-engined 14-seat feederliner, developed as the Miles Marathon.
- Type 5B – An eight-seat replacement for the biplane de Havilland Dragon Rapide, which gave rise to the DH Dove.

Often included in the Barbazon types purely due to it appearing in the same timeframe rather than actually being part of the Brabazon recommendations, is the Saunders Roe SR.45 Princess flaying boat. This was born of Ministry of Supply thinking that a replacement for the 1930s Shorts Empire and G Class flying boats would be needed for both Empire and transatlantic routes, and a proposal for a large new passenger flying boat was duly issued.

Through sheer size alone, the most high-profile aircraft here were the Bristol Brabazon and the Saunders-Roe SR.45 Princess flying boat. Both were huge aircraft and undoubtedly triumphs of engineering. The Brabazon was one of the largest aircraft in the world when it flew in 1949, while the Princess is still the largest all-metal flying boat ever built. Ultimately, however, both were failures. The industry was supposed to be moving on from carrying limited numbers of passengers in the lap of luxury (or it was before Concorde arrived), especially when it came to the transatlantic route for which the Brabazon was designed. As for the Princess, land-based aircraft could now do multi-stop journeys without the need for boat tenders and overnight stays, though the new routes definitely lacked the luxury and glamour of the 1930s Imperial Airways' flying boat service. Moreover, airlines no longer wanted ocean liner-style travel, they wanted to put as many passengers on a plane as possible to make the services profitable, with the heady 'jet set' days for transatlantic flights just around the corner, first with the de Havilland Comet, and greatly expanding when the Boeing 707 and Douglas DC-8 arrived.

For the smaller aircraft to meet Brabazon Type 2A definition, anything trying to contest the same arena as surplus DC-3 / C-47s was always going to struggle, especially if it was piston-engine. Consequently, only 23 Airspeed Ambassadors were built in an attempt to try replace the Dakota in the 'feederliner' arena, though these did linger a while longer than most contemporaries, with the last one retired by Dan-Air in 1971. Designed initially to compete in the same field, but with the then new turboprop engines, the Vickers Viscount fared much better. With more than 400 built it is the most successful British designed-and-built airliner and was used worldwide, though the Viscount's success was in part due to it becoming larger than the original Brabazon Type 2B requirement for 32 seats. At the suggestion of British European Airways (BEA), which originally bought the 47-seat Ambassador, the Viscount was to be stretched to accept at least the same number. The other key element of the Viscount's success was the decision to use Roll-Royce Dart turboprop engines, which proved to be very reliable, easily maintainable and had sufficient development potential to provide increased power output to suit this stretched, and later even higher capacity version of the Viscount, with some models having up to 86 seats.

Going up in size but down in volume manufactured, Bristol built 82 Britannias, with another 62 built under license by Canadair as the CL-28 Argus or as the CL-44. The Britannia, like the Princess, was designed for the Empire routes and also the transatlantic route for BOAC. Although 25 were ordered by BOAC in 1949, delays caused by problems with the Proteus turboprop engines and then the loss of the second prototype in 1953 due to an engine fire meant it failed to arrive in service until 1957. A year later, it began competing with jet-powered Comet 4s, followed by the first American jets, leading to a short operating life with BOAC on that route.

The Britannia found fortune elsewhere, however, as RAF Transport Command operated 20 mixed passenger/freight versions until the mid-1970s and among other overseas operators, it was used by

A British classic, the prototype VC10, G-ARTA, in the colours of British Overseas Airways Corporation (BOAC), probably when displayed at Farnborough in 1962. It features the unmistakeable shapes of 111 Squadron's Black Diamonds display team, Hunters, in the background.

The second production Vickers Viscount G-ALWF, now preserved at Duxford in 1950s BEA colours.

Cuba's national airline Cubana until 1990, as well as Aeronaves de Mexico, Canadian Pacific and Ghana Airways.

One operating sector that the Brabazon Committee inadvertently predicted was the growth of the feederliner. These are smaller passenger aircraft that are able to get into the out-of-the-way, little used, often shorter runway airports unsuited to larger aircraft, and return the passengers to the larger hub airports for connections to worldwide destinations. One aircraft that was designed to meet the Type 5A requirement was the Miles/Handley Page Marathon, which first flew in 1946. It saw very limited success as a civilian aircraft, and had a brief career as a navigational trainer for the RAF, but such was its unreliability that all had disappeared by 1959.

Much more successful, and designed to meet the Type 5B requirement as a replacement for the popular 1930s DH Dragon Rapide biplane, was the DH.104 Dove. With eight to 12 seats, and powered by a pair of DH Gypsy Queen piston engines, it sold well worldwide, with more than 500 built, and saw service with both civil and military operators, the RAF/Royal Navy (RN) called it the Devon and Sea Devon respectively. A modified version optimised for antipodean flying conditions was built by de Havilland Australia with a third engine in the nose. It was called the Drover, and became the workhorse of the Flying Doctor Service for several years.

The potential in the original design also allowed for some growth and a fuselage stretch plus the addition of a second pair of engines to produce the DH.114 Heron, which eventually saw a quite reasonable 149 built. Again, the type saw worldwide civilian and military sales, the RAF operating two in Queen's Flight colours for many years and the Royal Navy fielding five for communications and light transport duties

A sad end. The second Britannia prototype, G-ALRX, following its unscheduled encounter with the mud flats of the River Severn. After an exceptional display of piloting skill by Bristol's chief test pilot Bill Pegg, all those onboard walked away. Recovery efforts were greatly hindered by the tide swamping the aircraft.

The cockpit section of G-ALRX survives at Aerospace Bristol.

Newark Air Museum's DH.114 de Havilland Heron 1B G-ANXB in 1960s BEA livery. The Heron 1 prototype, G-ALZL, was dismantled and shipped to Australia, registered as VH-CJS and is now at Moorabbin Air Museum awaiting renovation.

as the Sea Heron. Like the Dove, modified versions also appeared, the most recognisable being those from Saunders in Canada as the ST-27, in which the four Gypsy Queen engines were replaced by a pair of Pratt & Whitney PT-6 turbo-props.

The stand-out aircraft emerging from the Brabazon types was the DH.106 Comet, the world's first jet-powered airliner. First flying on 27 July 1949, the natural metal finish of the Comet 1, its slightly swept-wing leading edges and four DH Ghost engines buried in the wing roots looked a world away from what had gone before and pointed the way to the future, with Britain leading the way.

Sadly, the euphoria did not last long. Once commercial service began in 1952, there were two crashes within six months of each other. On 26 October 1952, G-ALYZ failed to gain altitude immediately after take-off from Rome and suffered a heavy landing that thankfully all on-board survived. The second incident happened in March 1953, when a Canadian Pacific Airlines Comet 1A crashed killing all 11 on board. This led to changes in the wing design. Both crashes highlighted a problem with airflow to the engines causing loss of thrust should the pilot pitch the aircraft above the recommended angle for take-off. Worse was to come. On 2 May 1953, a BOAC flight out of Calcutta crashed in severe weather soon after take-off, with the loss of 43 lives. Much of the aircraft was recovered and taken to Farnborough for examination, and the subsequent inquiry pointed at over-stressing of the aircraft as a result of the pilot trying to maintain control in the high winds of the storm, which led to the loss of both wings.

On 10 January 1954, the first production Comet, G-ALYP, broke up in mid-air over the Mediterranean only 20 minutes after leaving Rome, killing all 35 onboard. As a result, BOAC grounded the Comet fleet while investigations were carried out. However, despite de Havilland engineers suggesting tens of modifications to cover potential design flaws, flights eventually continued.

The final act came only three months later, on 8 April 1954, when G-ALYY crashed into the sea near Naples, taking all 21 onboard with it. The Comet's certificate of air worthiness was cancelled, BOAC's fleet was placed in storage and the Royal Navy was again tasked with retrieval of the wreckage. The court of enquiry chaired by Lord Cohen and led by the director of the RAE at Farnborough, Sir Arnold Hall, eventually traced the cause of the aircraft lost in at least two of the crashes to metal fatigue brought on by the repeated stressing and de-stressing of the fuselage as it was pressurised on take-off and de-pressurised on landing. This was discovered only after a huge water tank was built at Farnborough to accommodate Comet G-ALYU that BOAC had donated for testing. The aircraft was subjected to repeated cycling of the cabin pressurisation system and eventually cracked open. Further detective work also revealed problems with the method of riveting used in construction that had accentuated the chances of fatigue. Having square, as opposed to round, windows also was found to increase the level of stress in the area of fuselage around them, each corner being a potential point of stress.

Regaining a certificate of air worthiness took four years of hard work from de Havilland, with a number of readily obvious and far more hidden changes made to how the Comet was built. Finally returning to service with BOAC as the Comet 4, the airliner was immediately used for the inaugural transatlantic jet passenger service on 4 October 1958. The new version with slightly longer fuselage, and round windows, also saw the original DH Ghost engines replaced with more powerful and fuel-efficient Rolls-Royce Avons. To many, it looked even better than the original. For the airlines, the benefits were also obvious, the passenger capacity had doubled, while the range and the cruising speed had also increased. With 114 built of all marks, the Comet 4 regained sales lost after the inevitable cancellations of the earlier version. The last Comet 4 departed UK civilian service with Dan-Air in 1981. However, in the four years the Comet was absent from the marketplace, Boeing introduced the 707 and Douglas the DC-8. Control of the airliner market had passed across the Atlantic.

DH.106 Comet 1 prototype G-ALVG at take-off, highlighting the unusual, single large main undercarriage wheels and the square-windowed fuselage.

Although the Comet was the first civilian passenger airliner, its lasting legacy was to benefit every other aircraft builder worldwide. It spurred on the introduction of a whole range of testing methodologies that made aircraft safer, refined the concept of fatigue in metals, and brought about the introduction of in-depth post-crash investigations. Boeing and Douglas said, at the time, that every aircraft manufacturer owed a debt of gratitude to de Havilland for this alone, but 114 lives was a high price to pay for progress.

Away from the civil arena, the Comet had another life in the RAF and with the RAE. After operating the Comet 2 in various guises including as transport, electronic signals intelligence platform (SIGINT), and testbed, the RAF eventually introduced the Comet-derived but much-modified Nimrod into service in 1969. It came to be regarded as a world-class anti-submarine warfare and maritime reconnaissance aircraft, serving with the RAF until 2011.

The Avro Ashton's roots can be traced back to one of the four interim types proposed by the Brabazon Committee, the Avro Tudor, though the Ashton was not built to be an actual commercial aircraft, but rather a research platform. With the lineage ultimately going back to the Avro Lincoln bomber, the Tudor was supposed to fill in as a transatlantic airliner prior to the Bristol Brabazon arriving and on the Empire routes pending the eventual appearance of the Bristol Britannia. It was less than successful on all counts, losing out to the Lockheed Constellation and the Douglas DC-4 on the American route.

The Tudor wasn't particularly well received in general; the tailwheel format was already regarded as passé for civilian use, while the design suffered from stability issues and had poor fuel economy. However, the Tudor was the first British civilian aircraft with a pressurised cabin. Sadly, the prototype

Jet-age beauty: Middle East Airlines Comet 4C.

The mighty hunter; former 50 Squadron Nimrod MR.2 XV250. The double bubble fuselage allowed Hawker Siddeley to give the Nimrod the extra space needed for the search radar and a versatile bomb bay, while allowing the retention of much of the existing Comet 4 airframe. Replacing the Avon engines with much more efficient Speys provided an un-refuelled range of more than 5,000 miles. (Craig Vaughton, courtesy Yorkshire Air Museum)

Tudor II, G-AGSU claimed the life of Roy Chadwick, designer of the Lancaster and the Vulcan, along with the rest of the crew, when it crashed on 23 August 1947.

The first Ashton was Ashton 1 WB490, which had been converted from the only Avro Tudor 8 built (VX195), itself a modification from a Tudor 1. Unlike the Tudor though, the Ashton was jet-powered, with a streamlined double nacelle under each wing housing Rolls-Royce Nene 5 engines, though future aircraft would all use Nene 6, each producing 5,000lb of thrust. Despite WB490 being jet-powered, it retained the tailwheel undercarriage of the Tudor, which placed the Nene jet pipes rather close to the ground, and all later aircraft were altered to use a tricycle undercarriage. In addition to the Tudor 8 used for WB490, the remaining surplus Avro Tudor 2 airframes were used to produce the six Ashtons built, all at Avro's factory at Woodford in Cheshire.

The complete production run for the Ashton comprised one Ashton 1, 2 and 4, and three Ashton 3s.

The space offered by engine nacelles designed for centrifugal-flow Nenes proved to be ideal for fitting slimmer axial-flow engines, and Ashton 2 (WB491) was used by Rolls-Royce for testing both Avon and Conway engines, as well as by Bristol Siddeley for Sapphires, with a Nene in one nacelle giving way to the type under test, all predominantly for engine de-icing trials.

Bristol Siddeley employed WB493, one of the trio of Ashton 3s built for Olympus engine testing with reheated units mounted in the outer nacelles. Later, the same aircraft was used for Orpheus testing. The Ashton 4 and all three Ashton 3s were also equipped with underwing bomb panniers and carried out a variety of both visual- and radar-assisted bombing research trials.

Newark Air Museum has the only surviving section from this half-dozen rather unique aircraft, the forward fuselage of Ashton 2 WB491.

Avro Ashton 1, WB490.

Ashton II WB491 at Newark Aviation Museum.

Above and right: **Two more views of what remains of the Ashton II WB491 at Newark, which also shows the rear of the cabin pressure cell.**

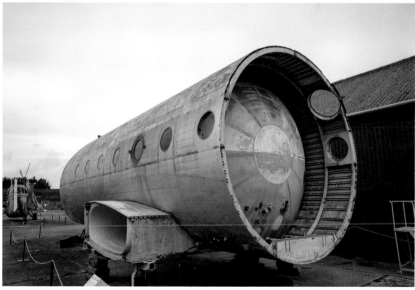

Chapter 5

Hawker P.1052 and the Hunter

The Royal Navy finally joined the jet age in 1950 with the Supermarine Attacker, though Hawker's first jet-powered design, the P.1040 Sea Hawk, which followed in 1953, soon began to replace it. Alongside the de Havilland Sea Venom, it relegated the Attacker to the reserve by 1957.

Despite being built to Air Ministry specification E38/46 to research swept-wing design, the P.1052 was the next step in the evolution of the Hawker family tree following the Sea Hawk, and the lineage becomes clear when the two are compared. The P.1052 retains the Sea Hawk wing root air intakes for the Rolls-Royce Nene engine, along with the bifurcated jet pipes and the straight-tail empennage, but more significantly, it was fitted with 35-degree swept wings. The remaining P.1052 is stored at the Fleet Air Arm's reserve collection in Cobham Hall, unfortunately without the major change from the Sea Hawk attached. As part of the design, Hawker introduced the option for the company to gather pressure-plotting data from the P.1052 wings, a first in any swept-wing aircraft and crucial to advance overall knowledge for implementation in future designs. P.1052 also incorporated the first appearance of pressure-relief doors in the engine intake to boost slow speed thrust. These were suggested by a new employee on Hawker's design team, Ralph Hooper, an engineer whose name and pressure doors appear later in the P.1127 family.

First flown on 19 September 1948, the first P.1052, VX272, was joined by a second prototype, VX279, in April 1949. VX272 underwent several changes over the next four years or so, gaining strengthened wings and fuselage, a variable incidence tail plane, an arrester hook to allow deck-landing trials (on HMS *Eagle* in May 1952), as well as the tail-plane bullet fairing just about visible in the photos. A heavy landing curtailed any further use, however, and the aircraft was removed from service in September 1953.

Changes to the second P.1072 VX279 in 1950 were so significant as to warrant a new designation P.1081, and this is the missing link between the P.1052 and the Hunter. While retaining the same nose and Nene engine as the Sea Hawk and P.1052, P.1081 incorporated a redesigned fuselage aft of the engine bay and replaced bifurcated jet pipes with a new straight-through jet pipe, which was found to improve available thrust, potentially with sufficient space to accommodate an afterburner. More significantly, P.1081 incorporated swept-tail surfaces, greatly improving flight characteristics into the high subsonic region, around Mach 0.95. So significant was this improvement that it was latterly applied to VX272.

Even with the straight tailplane fitted, and certainly once the swept tail was adopted, had the RAF, Royal Navy or the Ministry of Supply had a little foresight, the performance of the P.1052 should have indicated it could have made a good interim fighter before the Hunter arrived, though a full production version could not have been delivered early enough to be pitted against MiG-15s in Korea.

A fully developed P.1081 could also have provided the RAF with a home-grown aircraft rather than the eventual 11 squadrons of Canadair-built Sabres provided under the NATO Mutual Aid Program, which served predominantly in Germany until the Hunter arrived in 1954. The Australian government was, for a time, considering buying and producing the P.1081, powered by an improved and reheated version of the Nene, called the Tay, but opted for the 'old' and trusted Meteor F8 due

Seen on 'Flight Deck' at the Fleet Air Arm (FAA) Museum, Royal Naval Air Station Yeovilton, the Hawker Sea Hawk, which entered Royal Navy service in 1953.

to the urgent need to replace P-51 Mustangs currently in action in Korea. The Royal Australian Air Force (RAAF) later also bought North American F-86F Sabres, powered by Rolls-Royce Avon engines and much-modified by Commonwealth Aircraft Corporation; they went on to enjoy nearly 20 years of service.

As for the Royal Navy, it also looked at the P.1081 as a naval fighter, but the old guard of the battleship era failed to take the chance to operate a better fighter than the RAF possessed, and a swept-wing aircraft did not enter naval service until the arrival of the Scimitar in 1958.

The only instance of the P.1081 provided a great deal of data towards the eventual Hunter design, before it crashed on 3 April 1951, killing test pilot and Battle of Britain ace Squadron Leader 'Wimpy' Wade.

Despite the government believing there would be no war for ten years, the Air Ministry speculated that replacements for the Meteor and Vampire would be needed sooner rather than later, and specification F.43/46 was issued in 1946[4] calling for a new day-fighter for the RAF. Two years later, a night-fighter specification to replace the Meteor NF series, F.4/48, resulted in the Gloster Javelin, as well as the DH.110, which became the Sea Vixen under a further specification, N.14/49 (N for naval).

Gloster Aircraft submitted three designs for F.43/46, with one, the P.250, looking very similar to what later became the Javelin. Supermarine submitted the V-tailed Type 508, which eventually evolved into

---

4   F for Fighter, 43 representing the 43rd specification issued for all types that year and 46 for the year.

P.1052 in flight, same fuselage as the Sea Hawk, but swept wings.

One of only two Hawker P.1052 built, XV272 now resides in the Fleet Air Arm's reserve collection at Cobham Hall, a short distance from the main Yeovilton FAA museum.

A lack of space in Cobham Hall means the XV272 is stored with the wings detached.

the Scimitar. Sir Sydney Camm at Hawker submitted a simple-looking swept-wing design with a circular fuselage housing a similar Rolls-Royce Avon, to that fitted in the Canberra, which was designated as the P.1067. After further revision of the original specification, becoming F.4/48, which demanded a higher top speed, faster climb to height and four 30mm cannon, Camm and Hawker delivered what was christened the Hunter. It became the most successful post-war British fighter in terms of numbers built, with 1,972 constructed and sales to more than 20 countries, some using the type into the 1990s.

Longer than expected development issues saw the Hunter belatedly arrived in RAF service in July 1954, serving firstly as a day fighter as per the original requirement, replacing the Meteor, Venom and loaned Canadair Sabres on the front line of the Cold War in Germany. Although declared operational, the Avon engines proved troublesome, with engine surging and stalls the most common complaint, a problem exacerbated when firing the Aden cannons as the resultant gasses were ingested into the engine. Another issue with the Aden guns were the spent links that join each round to the next, which could cause fuselage damage when ejected. The cure for this was to fit a pair of blisters behind the gun bays to collect the links, giving the Hunter one of its characteristic features (christened 'Sabrinas' after a popular female film star of the time). Despite the Avon engine problems and the Hunter F2 arriving in service fitted with Armstrong-Siddeley Sapphire engines, the RAF eventually decided to retain the Avon and pursue Rolls-Royce for development of that, which eased spares and maintenance support in the process.

Further development of the Hunter led to several versions being introduced. Criticised for its short endurance in the early marks, the F.4 had additional tankage and wing strengthening as well as wing hard points for external stores. The F.6 delivered major updates, some of the changes resulting from cancellation of the P.1083 (see below). A total of 620 were produced, including licensed production for the Dutch and Belgian air forces. The F.6 also saw the introduction of a dog-toothed wing leading edge to cure pitching up issues. Additional fuel tankage was created in the wings using bag tanks and an additional pair of wing hard points were introduced. Better still, Rolls-Royce delivered the greatly improved, more powerful Avon 203 engine with 10,000lb of thrust for better performance, as well as increased fuel efficiency. The later FGA.9s were all converted from F.6s, again strengthening wings in the process, with the Air Staff finally approving the 100-gallon drop tanks attached to the inner wing hard points that Hawker had originally proposed for the F.4, which again increased flying time. With the Hunter starting to be displaced as a day fighter by the arrival of the considerably faster missile-armed Lightning, it was converted to the ground-attack role. The Hunter FR.10 also replaced the Supermarine Swift FR.5 in Germany as the RAF's photo-reconnaissance platform, with 33 converted from F.6s, with the addition of three F.95 cameras in the nose and fitment of 230-gallon drop tanks.

A trainer version, the T.7, was produced and had its first flight in October 1957; it incorporated a widened nose section that allowed a two-seat, side-by-side cockpit format. It was first built on F.4 specification airframes, though designers later adopted the dog-toothed wing leading edge of the F.6. The T.7 became a highly versatile basis for further marks of Hunter, including the T.7A, which was equipped with the flight systems from the Buccaneer and used as a conversion trainer. Furthermore, the T.8 for the Royal Navy had an added arrestor hook; it was only used on airfields and not stressed for carrier

The missing link, Hawker P.1081, built from the second P.1052, VX279, showing the 35 swept wings first seen on the P.1052, but also the swept tail and straight through jet pipe. The classic lines of the Hunter that followed are readily apparent.

P.1081 poses for the camera. Could it have been Britain's Sabre? Rolls-Royce Nene- or Tay-powered, cannon-armed and good handling, the potential was there.

Newark's T7, XL618, one of several T.7s still surviving, both on display and in flying condition (photographed prior to being repainted in 2024).

P.1067, Hawker Hunter F1 at Newark Air Museum. This was a hugely popular aircraft with pilots and gained major overseas sales.

landings; and the T.8M, which gained a new nose in order to house the Blue Fox radar from the FRS1 Sea Harrier and was used as a systems trainer, there being no two-seat Sea Harrier fitted with this radar.

Overseas sales generated a whole raft of additional mark numbers, but all were based on the main F.4, F.6, FGA.9 and T.7 versions operated by the RAF and Royal Navy. India was the biggest customer, taking 160 aircraft, using them operationally against neighbouring Pakistan on several occasions, where they came up against assorted MiGs and F-104s. Switzerland was close behind, buying 88 F.6/Mk.58 fighters and 52 FGA.9/Mk.58A ground-attack aircraft. Swiss Air Force Hunters were also some of the last to be relieved of front-line duties, finally bowing out in 1994. Over the years, Swiss Hunters also became some of the most capable, including fitment of AIM-9 Sidewinder air-to-air missiles, plus AGM-65 Maverick missiles for the ground-attack role. The Swiss Air Force also formed a popular aerobatic display team around the Hunter, Patrouille Suisse, painted in a patriotic brilliant red and white scheme of the Swiss flag, though nobody has yet to eclipse the world record display by the RAF's Black Arrows at Farnborough Air Show in 1958, looping 22 Hunters.

Hunter sales really did span the globe, with 19 countries adopting the aircraft, from Singapore in Asia, four European air forces, several operators in the Middle East, three in Southern Africa and across to Chile and Peru in South America. The flying qualities, reliability and ease of maintenance of the Hunter all contributed to this popularity. Demand for attrition replacements grew and so too did the customer base to the extent that, rather too late in the day and long after production had ceased, BAe suggested that if it was possible to create 200 or so additional Hunters, it could sell each one.

In 1953, however, one major opportunity in Hunter evolution was missed. Even Sir Sydney Camm could not persuade the board of Hawker Aviation to provide company funds and carry development of the P.1083 to flying status, just to see how well it flew. P.1083 was to be a Hunter with a 50-degree sweep 'thin wing' and a drag-reducing 'area ruled' fuselage, with power coming from a reheated Avon engine, resulting in an aircraft capable of sustained supersonic flight, as opposed to the barely transonic speed of the standard version.

Though it was initially seen as purely a research aircraft, it was viewed by the RAF as having production potential for service use in a short timescale, certainly before the Lightning arrived. While the Air Staff deliberated, Hawker's biggest worry was where to find room for more fuel, especially with a thirsty reheat now available, in an aircraft already struggling with short endurance. Delays in getting the Hunter into service led the Air Staff to officially cancel P.1083 in June 1953, pushing Hawker to resolve development issues with the standard model and incorporate certain elements of the P.1083 into what would become the F.6.

One particular Hunter deserves special mention. As well as being the first prototype, WB188 was modified by Hawker into the unique Mk3 specification aircraft solely to attempt to set the world air speed record. This it duly achieved, piloted by Hawker's chief test pilot, Squadron Leader Neville Duke on 7 September 1953, setting the record at 727.63mph over the sea near Littlehampton.

Changes to the original aircraft included a more pointed nose, reheated Rolls-Royce Avon engine, additional fuel tanks and strangely, air brakes, which the original aircraft lacked, though the rear fuselage side-mounted pattern found on the Mk3 and subsequently incorporated into early production aircraft was later replaced with a single ventral unit.

WB188 now resides at Tangmere Military Aviation Museum.

WB188 now sits resplendent in world air speed record livery at Tangmere Military Aviation Museum.

Midland Air Museum's F.6A XF382 in the markings of 234 Squadron, which was part of No 1 Tactical Weapons Unit at RAF Brawdy.

Norfolk and Suffolk Aviation Museum's FGA9, XG254, catches the late afternoon sun.

Chapter 6

Avro 707 and the V Bombers

The trio of aircraft dubbed the 'V Bombers' or 'V-Force', the Vickers Valiant, Handley Page Victor and Avro Vulcan, are intrinsically woven into the story of post-war British aircraft development and the UK's desire to have an independent nuclear deterrent, in parallel with the means to deliver it.

In among the myriad of designs to meet Air Ministry, Air Staff ORs or Air Staff Targets (ASTs), most of which never made it off a drawing board, OR.229 and OR.239 both appeared in 1946, calling for a high-altitude jet bomber able to deliver a single 'special' (ie, nuclear) weapon. That this weapon had yet to be developed, let alone tested, underlines how determined the government was to achieve this goal. OR.229 distilled into an Air Ministry Specification B.35/46, which called for an advance aircraft able to carry a single 10,000lb bomb at 55,000ft or more, at 500 knots, with a radius of action of 2,000 miles. Meanwhile, given the advanced nature of the specification, OR.239 became B.14/46, a less ambitious aircraft should the aircraft industry not be able to produce aircraft to meet B.35/46.

Short Sperrin

The aircraft built for B.14/46, the Short Sperrin, was little more than a piston-engine design that had replaced the piston engines with turbojets and had an airframe large enough to carry a single 10,000lb nuclear weapon.

A Short Sperrin with an enlarged lower engine intake on the port wing to accommodate testing of the 15,999lb-thrust DH Gyron turbojet. The three remaining nacelles housed Rolls-Royce Avons of a more modest 6,000lb.

With a maiden flight on 10 August 1951, but knowing that the Vickers Valiant had already beaten it into the air by three months, the government decided the less advanced aircraft was not needed and only two were built, VX158 and VX161. Converted to research aircraft, the two Sperrin proved useful aircraft as engine test beds. The size and construction of the engine nacelles make them highly adaptable. This allowed safe operation of the aircraft, initially with three standard engines, plus a test engine in the lower half of the engine nacelle on the port wing; XV158 appeared at the 1955 SBAC show at Farnborough in such a configuration, with three Avons and a single de Havilland Gyron. Later, both lower nacelles were modified to house a pair of different engines. Having a fully operational bomb bay, XV161 undertook bomb release trials for differing bomb shapes in support of the *Blue Danube* nuclear weapon and *Blue Boar* TV-guided glide bomb.

Despite their apparent usefulness, both Sperrins had been scrapped by 1959.

Vickers Valiant

Had it not been for much lobbying by Vickers' chief designer George Edwards, there may well only have been two V-bombers. Arguing that his design was simpler and subsequently less risky than those from Avro and Handley Page, complete with a promise it would be available sooner, yet another specification, B.9/48, was written around what would become the Valiant.

Compared to the Victor and the Vulcan, the Valiant was a more conventional design, but at the same time still looked the part. Edwards and Vickers also proved good to their word and the first prototype Valiant flew on 18 May 1951, a mere 27 months after the contract had been issued by the Air Ministry. The slightly less advanced nature of the Valiant also meant that there was no need for flying scale aircraft to ensure wing forms behaved or determined how they handled at low or high speeds. Only two prototypes were built, though the first was lost in a crash following a fuel fire, and Squadron Leader Brian Foster was killed after ejecting and hitting the tail fin.

Commencing with 138 Squadron at RAF Gaydon, Warwickshire, on 1 January 1955, along with an Operational Conversion Unit (OCU), another nine squadrons operated the 104 Valiant constructed. In addition, one more Valiant prototype was built in 1953, the B.Mk2. This had a strengthened airframe optimised for low-level flight and was conceived for use as a Pathfinder for the main bomber force.

The B.Mk2, WJ954, looked impressive in its gloss black finish. It had fairings on the inner wings to house the undercarriage, necessitated by space lost during the main spar strengthening for the low-level role, though moving the undercarriage also allowed more fuel tank space. Additionally, a longer forward fuselage was needed to counter the fairings weight, and more powerful engines gave it better performance. Belatedly, the Air Ministry realised the pathfinder role, epitomised by the DH Mosquito in World War Two, was obsolete, new navigation aids making a dedicated Pathfinder force rather pointless. The 17 already ordered were cancelled due to budget cuts in 1955 and WJ954 was scrapped in 1958, finding its way to what effectively became the cancelled aircraft graveyard, the gunnery ranges at Shoeburyness on the Suffolk coast.

By 1957, greatly improved Soviet air defences, especially following the shooting down of Gary Powers' U2 spy plane by Soviet missiles, highlighted that the days of high-level bombers were over and low-level attack became the order of the day for the whole of the V-Force, something the Mk1 Valiant was not designed to do. The cancellation of the Mk2 unexpectedly came back to haunt the Air Ministry. During 1962, a series of structural tests on the Valiant fleet resulted in a drastic reduction of the expected fatigue life of the airframe. A crack in the main spar of an aircraft undergoing tests using rocket-assisted take-off packs at Boscombe Down further underlined the problem. From early 1964 onwards, main spar failures in at least three more Valiants led to a complete fleet inspection and the costs involved with a major rework programme to extend the service life prompted the government to retire the Valiant by 1969.

Resplendent in anti-flash white, the sole surviving complete Vickers Valiant XD818 at the RAF Museum Midlands.

Valiant B.2 WJ954, the only one manufactured, and by the time of its first flight in 1953, the order for another 17 had already been cancelled.

Overshadowed by the longer careers of the other two V-bombers, the Valiant has the distinction of being the last British aircraft to drop an atomic weapon. First, WZ366 dropped a *Blue Danube* fission bomb as part of Operation *Buffalo* testing in Australia during 1956, and then XD818 a thermonuclear 'hydrogen' device as part of Operation *Grapple* weapon tests on Christmas Island in 1957. Appropriately, XD818, is the lone complete survivor.

Handley Page Victor

By 1950, at Handley Page, the HP.80 had become the recognisable shape of the Victor. Designers had endowed it with a beautiful crescent-shaped wing, once described as 'probably the most efficient high-subsonic wing of its time'. To test the wing, initially a one-third-scale glider was built, the HP.87, while a larger version of the wing shape was fitted to a highly modified Supermarine Attacker, becoming HP.88 VX330. Unfortunately, the HP.88 lasted two months before it crashed on 26 August 1951, after breaking up in flight, taking with it Handley Page test pilot D.G. Broomfield. The HP.88 would ultimately have contributed very little data to the main HP.80/Victor programme, predominantly due to the time it had taken to actually build the HP.88. In the interim, the wing shape of the HP.80 had changed to such an extent that any results from flying the HP.88 would have been unrepresentative of the final aircraft anyway.

Officially arriving in RAF service in 1958, the graceful lines of the production Victor B.1 provided a superb high-altitude, long-distance strike aircraft. Despite this, an even higher operational ceiling was now demanded by the RAF and plans for two upgraded versions were presented by Handley Page. Initially, the B.2 was intended to be powered by a higher thrust Armstrong Siddeley Sapphire Mk9 as opposed to the Mk7 found in the B.1. The B.3 involved more extensive changes, including an increased wingspan, along with either similar Bristol Siddeley Olympus engines to the Vulcan, or Rolls-Royce Conways, both of which required changes to the air intakes to accommodate increased airflow. With the cancellation of the Mk9 Sapphire, Handley Page opted for the Conway to power what amounted to

Victor prototype WB771, tragically lost on 14 July 1954, along with all onboard.

Victor K2 XL231 *Lusty Linda* in the autumn gloom. Formerly of 57 Squadron, after taking part in much of the development of the K2 tanker programme, XL231 returned to service as a K2 in 1977, later participating in the Falklands conflict and finally the first Gulf War, for which its camouflage scheme was painted. (Courtesy Yorkshire Air Museum)

something approaching halfway between the B.2 and B.3. It was modified to allow new engines but had the same wing length. The RAF accepted this into service to avoid any delays in waiting for a full B.3 development.

The Victor went on to faithfully serve the RAF until 1998, initially as a strategic bomber, but once the switch was made to low-level strike, a role for which the crescent wing design proved far too fragile, it was as a strategic reconnaissance aircraft, and crucially as an air-to-air refuelling tanker. The famous *Black Buck* missions during the 1982 Falklands War would have been impossible without the exploits of 55 and 57 Squadrons' Victor tankers. During that campaign, ten aircraft were needed to get the single Vulcan used to carry out each raid, with some close calls fuel wise even on the successful missions. Continued Falklands' resupply flights were all supported by Victors and the flying hours rapidly eroded the fatigue life of the fleet, greatly accelerating the need to find a replacement. Eventually, this was met by an already on-going VC10 conversion process, as well as the arrival of Lockheed Tristar tankers, though six Vulcans were also converted to single-point tankers and pressed into service for a time.

Avro Vulcan

Across at Avro's Woodford facility near Manchester, in 1947, the Avro 698 project became the unmistakable delta-winged Vulcan. In adopting the delta platform, Avro required a great deal of information few companies in the UK possessed. It included the handling and flight characteristics of a tail-less, thick delta wing. A total of five one-third scale development Avro 707s were built to contribute data to the design programme within the low-speed regime. A half-sized Avro 710 was planned to explore the high-speed envelope. However, this was cancelled before it was built, considered too time consuming to produce, so a modified 707A variant was substituted in its place. The first 707 built, VX784, first flew in September 1949, but sadly crashed later the same month, killing test pilot Flt Lt Eric Esler.

The second 707, VX790, flew 12 months later, re-designated 707B and piloted by Wing Cmdr Roland 'Roly' John Falk. Falk later went on to pilot the Vulcan on its maiden flight on 30 August 1952.

The 707B differed from the original model, gaining a lengthened fuselage, increased wing sweep and a different cockpit canopy. As with the original 707, some of its constituent parts were donated from elsewhere. The 'new' canopy belonged to the Gloster Meteor; a longer nose oleo leg was borrowed from the Hawker P.1052 to raise the wing incidence on take-off or landing; and the main gear was acquired from the Avro Athena trainer. The raised undercarriage incidence became largely the only major contribution towards the 698 project, as the time taken to modify the 707B and build the later 707A reduced their usefulness.

The 707A, WD280, built to perform the high-speed trials originally meant for the cancelled Avro 710, arrived with wing root air intakes after problems with airflow into the dorsal intakes of the 707B, though the intake location did at least represent something more akin to those on the Vulcan. Later, the wings were modified to the same compound sweep leading edge adopted by the production Vulcan. Despite the prototype Vulcan having already flown, a second 707A was built to supposedly speed up the development programme.

The 707C, WZ744, was the last model to be produced and the only two-seater aircraft of the five, complete with dual controls. It was originally one of four ordered to act as familiarisation trainers, but the final three were cancelled, the Vulcan being deemed easy to fly without a dedicated trainer.

Avro 707A, WZ736 seen here when still at the Museum of Science and Industry in Manchester.

After the Vulcan progressed into service, the 707s continued to serve as excellent research aircraft in the UK for the RAE and, in the case of WD280, in Australia for use by the Aeronautical Research Laboratories.

Following two accidents in 12 months, the 707B, VX790, was used for spares and eventually broken up in 1960, while the two 707As built and the sole 707C all survive. WD280 remained in Australia and is at the Royal Australian Air Force (RAAF) Museum in Point Cook, Victoria. The other 707A, WZ736, spent years at the Museum of Science and Technology in Manchester, but moved to Boscombe Down Aviation collection at Old Sarum in 2022. After a period when the 707C was not on public display at the RAF Museum Midlands, it finally found its rightful home; the Avro Heritage Museum at Woodford.

The photos here show WZ736 and WZ744 in their former homes, WZ744 at RAF Museum Midlands and WZ736 in Manchester.

Head on 707C, looking every bit a miniature Vulcan.

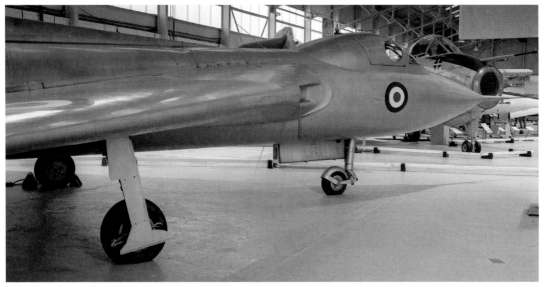

Side view of the only 707C built.

An interesting illustration of all the various Avro 707 versions, with the first built notably shorter in length.

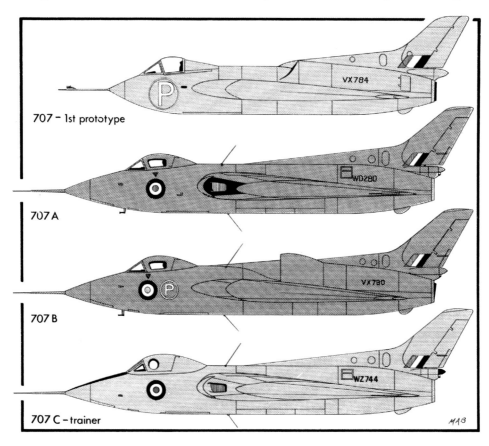

Originally envisioned as one of three lead-in trainers for pilots destined for the Vulcan, this is the only 707C built after a trainer was deemed unnecessary.

Often referred to as 'mother and chicks' when they flew overhead near the Avro plant at Woodford, the four 707 development aircraft with one of the Vulcan prototypes.

Above the clouds, a beautiful portrait of Vulcan prototype VX770. (*Aeroplane*)

Chapter 7

Over the Rainbow – Britain's Bomb

It seems appropriate here to diverge from aircraft to bombs and missiles, as for a time, Britain's ability to successfully develop a nuclear deterrent compact enough to be carried aloft by the RAF, greatly influenced the aircraft projects being built to deliver the device.

Despite Duncan Sandy's slightly mistaken beliefs that manned aircraft would be replaced by missiles, which resulted in the milestone 1957 Defence White Paper, to some extent and certainly in strategic terms, he was right, just a decade too early. The RAF's manned strategic bombers gave way to the Royal Navy taking ownership of the British nuclear deterrent, with the first patrol of HMS *Resolution* and its cargo of Polaris missiles happening in June 1968.

Yet even with its emphasis on missiles to replace manned fighters and bombers, the same White Paper cancelled work on a Mach 3 ramjet-powered weapon designed to destroy Soviet bombers and allocated

Awaiting resources for restoration and with all the makings of a very interesting display, Newark's Bloodhound missile with the associated Ferranti Type 86 'Firelight' fire control radar unit. At each side of the missile centre body are Bristol Thor ramjet sustainer motors, which provide the thrust for the main duration of flight.

RAF Museum Midlands' Bloodhound with a better view of the Thor ramjets (with brown nose cones) and the arrangement of the solid propellant boosters, which provide acceleration off the launcher, up to the point where the ramjets become effective, when the boosters detach.

the code[5] 'Blue Envoy'. A great deal of work was only saved after a number of informal suggestions from the companies developing Blue Envoy (Bristol Aircraft and Ferranti) to the Ministry of Supply that what had already been developed and the government had paid for, could be used to improve the 'Red Duster' missile currently starting production. Red Duster was later christened 'Bloodhound' and provided the RAF airfields that housed the V-bombers with the only high-altitude surface-to-air missile system Britain has ever deployed. Developments made it effective enough to serve into the early 1990s, when the bomber threat appeared to have gone. Bloodhound was sold to Switzerland, Sweden, Australia and Singapore. Based on Bloodhound, a similar shorter range, but semi-portable missile, Thunderbird, served with the British Army until 1977.

Bomber Command's problems with the nuclear deterrent started before a V bomber had even flown; all the designs were tied to the size and shape of a bomb intended to house the best nuclear device

---

5 The likes of 'Blue Steel', 'Red Dean', 'Blue Jay' the numerous other names littering post war British military projects are 'Rainbow Codes', a system of random names designed to conceal a project's actual use and a product of the Ministry of Supply (MoS). Their adoption officially ended along with the MoS in 1958, when the departments work was split with the War Office, Air Ministry (Military) and the Ministry of Aviation (Civil). Of course, this didn't stop the RAF christening the first batch of Foxhunter radar sets fitted to Tornado F2s 'Blue Circle'. This in reference to the original radar sets being as much use in their intended role, as the cement ballast weight from the cement company of the same name. These weights were fitted in the aircraft nose, when the radar sets were removed before a fully working Foxhunter radar unit was available

Norfolk and Suffolk Aviation Museum's Bloodhound Mk 1 with Ferranti fire control radar; the missile sits on the standard 'zero length' launcher.

Britain could produce, what would later be termed the 'physics package'. The 1946 US McMahon Act, which prevented export of atomic technology, even to allies, was a slap in the face to British wartime involvement. With all the collaborative work with the USA and Canada now lost, Britain faced the costly prospect of having to do it all again on its own. The trouble was, British scientists struggled to reduce the size of the physics package to the same extent their American counterparts had, resulting in the Blue Danube bomb being on the larger side to accommodate it and consequently, V bomber bomb bays had to be equally cavernous.

By 1954, four years before Britain had actually detonated a thermo-nuclear fusion type device, the Ministry of Supply realised that continued improvements in Soviet air defences, meant that the chances were reducing for any V bomber actually to get to the 50,000ft release altitude needed for 'Blue Danube' or its successors. Consequently, they looked at extending the effectiveness and longevity of the V-Force by having a stand-off weapon and instigated the design of a rocket-powered guided missile, housing a thermo-nuclear warhead.

The building of the missile was contracted to Avro, which had no prior experience of guided weapon design. Nevertheless, Blue Steel was duly born, and this was the name that it carried into service. At 35ft long and with a wingspan of 13ft, Blue Steel was actually of a similar size to the Shorts SR.53 mixed-power development aircraft, which naturally enough caused problems housing it under the Victor and Vulcan. The Valiant simply lacked the ground clearance to accept it. Although the Victor could take off with a Blue Steel underneath, the difficulties in loading it led to the Vulcan become the most viable carrying aircraft.

Propulsion was provided by a dual-chamber Armstrong Siddeley Stentor Mark 101 rocket motor, fuelled by high test peroxide (HTP) and kerosene; both chambers used for the initial Mach 1.5 boost,

'Yellow Sun', the designation for the actual bomb shape for Britain's first high yield nuclear weapon, a 400Kt physics package called 'Green Grass'. This was later replaced by a 1.1Mt device called 'Red Snow', which was based on the American W28 warhead once the McMahon Act was amended.

'Red Beard', the first tactical nuclear weapon design in Britain, which could be dropped from RAF Canberras and all the V bombers, as well as Royal Navy Scimitars, Buccaneers and Sea Vixens.

The last tactical nuclear weapon deployed to the RAF and RN, WE.177. It is small enough to be carried by anything from a Vulcan to a Sea Harrier, as well as RN anti-submarine helicopters ,which would have used the device as a depth bomb. All the display bombs are in the Cold War exhibition hall at the RAF Museum Midlands.

which ran for less than 30 seconds, and the smaller cruise engine took over for the duration of the flight and both then boosted the missile to Mach 3 nearer the target. By the time it became operational in February 1963, the problems with the size of the physics package had gone, the world political situation and Britain's successful H-Bomb tests had led the USA to amend the McMahon Act and the UK gained access to American weapon data, allowing the Atomic Weapons Establishment at Aldermaston to build 'Red Snow', a variant of the US W-28 warhead with a 1.1MT yield. The inertial navigation system onboard was designed to deliver the missile to within 500m of the desired target, with a designed range of around 185km; it should have given the RAF a very effective weapon, but it was less than satisfactory in reality.

Pre-flight preparation, including installing the warhead, which was never stored with the missile, took seven hours. The volatility of the propellent required ground crew to don special protective clothing during fuelling, usually accompanied by bowsers full of copious amounts of water to dilute the HTP, just in case. Furthermore, the RAF was unconvinced of the missile's general reliability or accuracy.

A Mk2 version with extended range and a ramjet engine had been cancelled before the Mk1 even entered service, but this was due to interest in another weapon.

With Royal Navy chiefs keen for Britain to acquire Polaris and consequently new nuclear submarines to go with it, RAF efforts to retain the deterrent led to early involvement with the United States Air Force (USAF) and the Douglas AGM-48 Skybolt air-launched ballistic missile programme. This included Vulcans being assigned to the USA for a time to complete airframe compatibility and release trials. Unlike Blue Steel, which took a direct line to the target over a comparatively short range, with a quick climb phase close to the target, followed by a descent to the detonation point, Skybolt took the long

Midland Air Museum's Blue Steel and a handy gauge of the missile length can be made by the 6ft fence panels behind.

route, with more than double the range and a ballistic trajectory. Guidance for Skybolt was an inertial platform that included a star tracker to get a definite fix prior to launch, a process that caused a great deal of trouble during development. Four failed test launches did the project no favours at all, but what became the final test was successful.

With the Americans already having silo-launched ballistic missiles, Minuteman had just started to supplement the earlier Titan, and with the success of the submarine-launched Polaris missile, despite lobbying from supporters of the USAF and Douglas, the Kennedy administration pulled the plug on Skybolt in December 1962, leading to a great deal of anger and later even more persuasion from the UK government to be supplied with Polaris in its place. This eventually paid off following lengthy negotiations, and the USA and the UK signed the Polaris Sales Agreement on 6 April 1963. Carriage of Britain's deterrent passed to the Royal Navy five years later and the V Force was reassigned to NATO under the terms of the agreement, carrying tactical nuclear weapons. Some voices at the time, and in the years since, have questioned the terms set out by the USA for UK operation of Polaris and later Trident, claiming it led to a less than truly independent deterrent.

The work on the Vulcan with Skybolt unexpectedly became useful almost 20 years later during the Falklands War in 1982. When planning for the *Black Buck* raids on Port Stanley runway and surrounding Argentine positions, questions were raised on the possibility of fitting anti-radiation missiles (ARMs) to Vulcans to take out Argentine air defence radars. Utilising the wiring and hard point locations originally installed for Skybolt, lateral thinking and customary engineering ingenuity allowed the fitment of AGM-45 Shrike ARMs transferred from USAF European stocks (weapons usually found on F4G 'Wild Weasel' Phantoms). As a result, Shrikes were successfully employed on at least two of the raids.

As for a silo-based strategic deterrent provided by rockets housed on the UK mainland, akin to the Minuteman missiles found in America's 'Missile Fields' in Dakota, or French S3 missiles formerly sited on the Plateau d'Albion, this had actively been investigated during the early 1950s. Four geologically stable sites had eventually been found for the proposed 'Blue Streak' intermediate range ballistic missile. This was before the government realised that Britain lacks the space for adequate separation of fixed launch sites from urban areas, without putting a large proportion of the population under increased threat from an attack on the silos. Escalating development costs, including expansion of the Woomera test site in Australia, coupled with those projected for building the UK launch facilities in the first instance, plus anticipated maintenance figures led to Blue Streak being cancelled in February 1960. Another reason British government attention then turned to the Douglas Skybolt as the UK deterrent.

The USA indirectly benefited from the cancellation of Blue Streak. UK engineers had started thinking early in the planning phase for Blue Streak deployment about the engineering requirements for housing and the effects of firing rockets from an enclosed space than their American counterparts had not considered. Consequently, many UK launch silo ideas and designs were adopted by the US government during the building of their numerous missile launch areas.

Right: **Newark Air Museum has a Stentor rocket motor from Blue Steel in its engine building. Note the huge difference in size between the main combustion chamber nozzle and the considerably smaller cruise nozzle.**

Below: **Semi-recessed under Vulcan B.2 XM572, Blue Steel Mk.1. (Crown copyright)**

As another indicator of size, this is the RAF Museum Midlands Blue Steel sat beside its Victor B2.

For comparison, a Douglas Skybolt under the wing of their Avro Vulcan B2.

Chapter 8

Vectored Thrust – V/STOL and the Evolution of the Harrier

Without doubt, the most unique aircraft to achieve operational status of all the prototypes of the 1950s and '60s, the Hawker Harrier stands proud. That it nearly didn't come to fruition should come as no surprise, though the gestation period and hurdles faced prior to its entry into service were protracted.

From the ungainly Rolls-Royce 'Flying Bedstead', through the Short S.C.1, to the more recognisable shapes of Hawker's P.1127 and Kestrel, the end result could have been a supersonic vertical and/or short take-off and landing (V/STOL) combat aircraft as envisaged by Hawker with the P.1154 in 1962. But, in the end, the RAF eventually gained a Hunter replacement in the Harrier GR.1 and went on to develop operational procedures to fully exploit the abilities of an aircraft able to take off from virtually anywhere. With the demise of the Royal Navy's sole remaining conventional aircraft carrier, HMS *Ark Royal*, in 1979, even the Navy came to love the Harrier, and both services thoroughly proved the aircraft during the Falklands campaign, nearly 15 years after the cancellation of P.1154.

The FAA Museum's P.1127, XP980. A careful look at the engine intakes shows it has lost the inflatable rubber lip unique to the early P.1127 and designed to smooth the airflow at slow speeds. The inflatable lips were replaced with a more conventional smooth metal combing due to concerns over in-service durability.

Rolls-Royce Thrust Measuring Rig: 'the Flying Bedstead'

Test vehicles can come in some strange forms, though usually one with wings would be expected to qualify as an aircraft. Rolls-Royce, however, had a definite set of criteria for its thrust-measuring rig (TMR), and wings were not required. One glance at the resultant machine and it's not hard to see why it soon gained the nickname 'the Flying Bedstead'.

Built of tube steel and powered by a pair of Nene engines mounted back-to-back, the TMR stood on four legs, with castor-type wheels on the ends to allow ground handling. Though the main lifting thrust was derived from the dual engine jet pipes directed down under the TMR centre body, control thrust came from nozzles on long arms, one on each side and one extending beyond each end of the main rig. Built at the Rolls-Royce test airfield at Hucknall in Nottinghamshire, it first flew from the site in August 1953, tethered to a specially built overhead frame and harness, which governed the size of the test area within which it could manoeuvre.

Equally as crucial to the success of the project as the engine thrust and attitude nozzles, was an electronic stabilisation system that had been built by the Royal Aircraft Establishment for the TMR. Electronics and sensors played a huge part in the life of the Harrier family, and the ability of the 'auto-stab' system to allow vertical landings in tough weather conditions began here.

A year of tethered flights finally led to the first free flight on 3 August 1954, with Rolls-Royce pilot Ronald Shepherd at the controls. Freed from the restraints of the tethering frame, the TMR was transferred firstly to RAE at Farnborough and then to RAE Bedford for further test flights, many investigating the capabilities of the auto-stabilisation system. Weather greatly affected the flying programme, and no flights were undertaken with wind speeds over 10 knots, and the rig as a whole was heavily reliant upon

The remaining Rolls-Royce thrust-measuring rig (TMR) hangs from the ceiling in the Science Museum and enables visitors to see the arrangement of main engine jet pipes under the centre body, ducting for the thruster outriggers and castor-wheeled undercarriage.

the auto-stab unit to maintain level flight. Not much comfort to the pilot, who was sat perched high on top of the test rig and whose only safety device was a roll-over bar. A second rig was built to expand the programme, but shortly after, the first TMR suffered a control system failure and crashed (the pilot escaped injury), the second rig later crashed and killed Wg Cdr H.G.F. Larsen while on his first test flight.

The TMR provided valuable information that directly led to future developments in the vertical take-off and landing projects as they evolved during the 1960s. Rolls-Royce used some of the data for the RB.108 lift engine, which was its first dedicated engine expressly aimed at providing thrust for VTOL aircraft. This engine and more of the data from the TMR went into the Short SC.1, where the RB.108 provided both vertical and horizontal thrust.

The arrangement of trust control nozzles on the arms at the extremities of the thrust rig were incorporated into the body of the Shorts SC.1 and later the Hunting H.126. In refined form, a similar system was also used on the P.1127, Pegasus and Harrier. Commonly referred to as 'puffer ducts', careful inspection of any of these aircraft will reveal a series of cleverly integrated, hydraulically actuated shutters shielding jet nozzles within or close to the wing tips, extreme nose, and on both sides as well as under the tail fairing.

These reaction control jets used bleed air from the main engine to control the aircraft's attitude when in the hover, assisted by the auto-stab system, provided with input from pressure and motion sensors, combined with the pilot's control input. Fitting jets directed both up and down on the wing tips improved roll stability when hovering, as they were set to be mutually opposed when operating port up with starboard down and vice versa. The nose and tail ducts provided pitch control, while the ducts on each side of the small tail boom provided the yaw control. Anyone who has witnessed a Harrier flying display will appreciate the effectiveness of this system.

TMR 'in flight'. It retains the frame over the cockpit from when it was attached to a harness during tethered flying tests. This also serves as a rudimentary form of crash rollover bar.

Opposite ends of the development spectrum. A Rolls-Royce TMR sits alongside a Fairey Delta FD.2.

Rolls-Royce RB.108 Vertical Lift Engine

When the idea of vertical take-off aircraft was first mooted, Rolls-Royce started looking at jet engines optimised just to provide lift. Ideally these should be built with components as light as possible, but mounted to run at an angle roughly 90 degrees to that of a conventional jet, and hence needed all the cooling and lubrication oil paths changed to suit primarily an upright operating position. This work resulted in the RB.108 research engine, a small, light, (4ft long, 267lb) turbojet that delivered 2,500lb of thrust.

Prior to a full test in the Shorts SC.1, Rolls-Royce acquired Gloster Meteor FR.9, VZ608, which had previously been modified for trials with a reheated engine system in longer nacelles. Modified again to accommodate a single RB.108 lift engine behind the cockpit, and in place of the main fuel tank, which was replaced by a pair of external tanks, though aircraft endurance was still reduced to just 30 minutes. A replica SC.1 air scoop was also fitted to check inlet air flow, and the RB.108 could be adjusted in flight to simulate running while delivering vertical lift. With tests completed, including an investigation into ground erosion from jet efflux, VZ608 was relegated to the fire dump at Rolls-Royce's Hucknall test centre. Rescued by Newark Air Museum in 1970 and after major renovation work during the mid-1990s following the discovery of serious corrosion, this little-known contributor to V/STOL flight research resides in Hangar 2 at Newark.

The RB.108 would eventually also fly in research aircraft from Vereinigte Flugtechnische Werke (VFW) and Dornier in Germany, but more notably in the Mirage Balzac V, France's research aircraft that led to the Mirage IIIV, the competitor to the Hawker P.1154 (see below).

Newark Air Museum's unique Meteor FR9 vertical and/or short take-off and landing (V/STOL) test bed. The Shorts SC.1-style air intake for VZ608 sits under the wing.

A closer look at the Rolls-Royce R RB108 lift engine. It is quite a compact unit compared to the standard RR Derwent of the Meteor.

The first Short SC.1, XG900, now mounted on a column in the Science Museum, London, and missing a wing. The engine air intakes have been removed and the fuselage has been braced to better display the 4 RB.108 lift engines.

Short SC.1

Slightly more orthodox in design than the TMR it followed, the Short SC.1 still presents a rather unusual profile compared to other aircraft. It was built to the 1953 Ministry of Supply requirement ER.143T, which called for a VTOL aircraft able to complete transitions from the hover to forward flight and from the hover to landing. Short Brothers opted to build a suitably lightweight airframe around five Rolls-Royce RB.108 turbojets. Four engines in the centre of the airframe provided vertical lift, with the remaining engine providing forward thrust. With the cockpit designed to optimise airflow over the top of the fuselage and into the engine air intakes, the polished natural metal finish and all-Perspex nose gives the aircraft a futuristic look even today. The limited power from the single cruise engine ensured all flight would be relatively low speed, allowing a fixed undercarriage to be used. As the rate of descent from the hover was something of an unknown, the undercarriage was capable of coping with quite high sink rates, as well as needing heat-resistant tyres due to the proximity of the lift engine efflux.

The single rear-mounted RB.108 cruise engine was incorporated into the base of the tail, the engine itself sitting at 45 degrees and the actual jet pipe for it cranked to exhaust along the aircraft thrust line. Ahead of this was a vented panel with an additional airflow deflector flap for the intakes to the gimbal-mounted lift engines. As became the norm, engine bleed air-fed controllable vents for slow speed control, especially in the hover, the most noticeable on the SC.1 were housed in the nose bump. Like the TMR, the SC.1 incorporated an auto-stabilisation control system, but the Short aircraft also became the first British aircraft to have a fly-by-wire control system, with pilot input and stabilising signals electrically transmitted to actuators for the control surfaces and nozzles.

The first prototype, XG900, took its first flight using a conventional take off on 2 April 1957, though with no lift engines installed. The first tethered vertical flight took place on 26 May 1958, and the transition from the hover to forward flight occurred on 6 April 1960. The SC.1 was displayed at both Farnborough and Paris, making the Channel crossing under its own power.

Sadly, on 2 October 1963, the second prototype XG905 crashed, killing pilot J.R. Green, with the accident attributed to a control malfunction. However, the aircraft was rebuilt and continued in use until 1967.

The SC.1 was very successful in increasing understanding of how aircraft perform at low speeds and the problems involved in transitioning from forward flight to the hover or the hover to forward flight. However, the biggest insight the Hawker development team took away from the RAE, after a visit in February 1959, was the benefits of the auto-stabilisation system.

Despite Rolls-Royce's best attempts at promoting lift engines for vertical take-off during the 1960s and '70s, the success of having a jet engine with thrust vectoring, negating the need to carry around dedicated lift engines that become a dead weight once forward flight is achieved, won the day, certainly in the West. Although Dassault in France produced two Mirage-based fighters with lift engines, in Germany, Dornier, EWR and VFW built transport aircraft and fighters utilising lift engines and vectored thrust engines, or in one case, rotating engine pods; none progressed further than being research aircraft. However, all of these progressed no further than development aircraft. The only aircraft to achieve operational service with lift engines was the Soviet Yak-38 'Forger' operated by the Soviet Navy aboard the Kiev Class ships, which the Soviets defined as 'heavy aircraft cruisers'. The follow-on Yak-141 'Freestyle' was designed as a supersonic replacement for the Yak-38, but the project was cancelled after only four aircraft were built.

Even though the Harrier's replacement in RAF and Royal Navy service, the Lockheed Martin F-35B, appears to use a lift engine, the front lift fan is shaft-driven from the main engine, while the single rear exhaust nozzle can articulate down through 90 degrees, and the two combined provide the thrust to achieve vertical take-off or landing.

XG900 resides in the Science Museum in South Kensington, while XG905 is preserved at the Ulster Folk and Transport Museum in Northern Ireland.

Short SC1 XG905 at the Ulster Folk and Transport Museum in Northern Ireland.

XG905 in the hover.

A closer look at XG905, showing the engine intake arrangements. The lift engines sit under the dorsal grilles, with the hinged forward section deploying for vertical flight to divert more air into the intakes than the grilles could provide. The rear intake for the forward thrust RB.108 sits behind these, at the base of the tail.

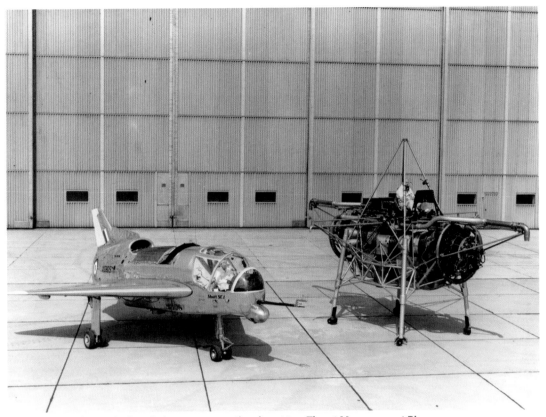

Progress. Short's SC.1 looks a little more conventional next to a Thrust Measurement Rig.

Hawker P.1154 and BS.100

Jet engine development often goes hand in hand with a new aircraft, though during the 1950s and '60s, engine development was one of the primary reasons a number of aircraft projects ran into lengthy delays. Bristol Siddeley's Olympus and Sapphire, de Havilland Engines' Gyron Junior and Rolls-Royce's Avon all had issues and caused problems for the aircraft designed to use them.

Bristol Siddeley's BS.53 Pegasus was fitted to the Hawker P.1127/Kestrel and finally saw exceptional service in the Harrier. The unique thrust-vectoring nozzles provided the means of achieving the amazing feats for which the Harrier became famous, including unrivalled air combat manoeuvrability, the ability to operate from virtually anywhere and wowing airshow crowds wherever it appeared.

The Harrier was subsonic, but what if it had been supersonic? The P.1127 demonstrated the possibilities of vectored thrust and hinted at the potential it offered, but at Hawker and Bristol-Siddeley plans were coming together for a more powerful engine and the aircraft to house it.

The standard Pegasus engine is not all that it seems. While it may be assumed that the thrust from the four nozzles is the same, this is not the case. The front nozzles are technically 'cold'; air from these does not go through the combustion chambers of the engine and is instead generated by the large diameter turbines of the low-pressure stages at the front of the engine. The rear 'hot' nozzles take the airflow from the post-combustion, high-pressure stages and operate at temperatures around 650 C or 720 C dependent upon whether water injection is enabled to cool the high-pressure stages, water injection being used primarily for combat and some landing or take-off situations. The 50 gallons of demineralised water carried lasts around 12 minutes, and the pilot receives audible warnings when it's running out.

In the same way as reheat boosts engine thrust when engaged, by controlled injection of fuel into an extended jet pipe, Plenum Chamber Burning (PCB) was designed to do that for the Pegasus, except it was far harder to achieve. PCB needed to inject, ignite and burn fuel where previously there was no need, ahead of the main combustion chambers of the engine and fuel injection into an already hot gas stream that isn't there.

Bristol Siddeley built the BS.100 to accommodate the PCB system and it resulted in a slightly larger and broader engine than Pegasus, which was largely due to it being based around an Olympus core rather than the Orpheus core of Pegasus. The Hawker Siddeley P.1154 would have been wider and longer than the Harrier in order to accommodate the larger engine, as well as to carry more fuel, the air-intercept radar, two pilots in the Royal Navy version and operational avionics.

P.1154 was born from NATO Basic Military Requirement 3 (NBMR-3), a competition initiated in July 1961 to find a VTOL combat aircraft to fulfil NBMR-3a for a fighter and 3b for a ground-attack aircraft. Conceived at a time when NATO realised that conventional airfields could easily be knocked out, it wanted an aircraft able to operate from anywhere. Just two designs were submitted, P.1154 and the French Mirage IIIV, though the single-engine simplicity of the British design was judged to have won on technical grounds. There was one caveat with this contest; there was no 'prize' money to build the aircraft, it was up to NATO member states to fund the winner to production, and, as is often the case with NATO, not one country actually produced an operational aircraft to meet NBMR-3, though the French at least saw the Mirage IIIV developed into a flyable prototype, but the project was cancelled after the second prototype crashed.

In the UK, inter-service rivalry did the plans for P.1154 no good at all. The Royal Navy had wanted to replace the Sea Vixen with the McDonald Douglas F4 Phantom for some time, as this also meant keeping large conventional aircraft carriers, but it reluctantly agreed to join the RAF in having the P.1154. The Air

One of few BS.100 engines built, now on display at the Fleet Air Arm Museum, RNAS Yeovilton.

BS.100 rear view, the normal hot end, with jet pipe sensor connectors arranged around the nozzle mounts.

Ministry hoped that once the RAF and Navy had essentially the same aircraft there would be cost savings thanks to the commonality of parts and economical number of airframes built. The trouble was that Navy requirements for a tricycle undercarriage, two seats, folding wings and nose to ease carrier hangar storage, as well as a different radar fit, eventually meant the Royal Navy dropped out to pursue the F-4 Phantom.

This left the RAF with the chance to acquire a supersonic V/STOL aircraft to its requirements and Hawker able to concentrate on designing it. However, the newly elected Labour government decided to cancel P.1154 on cost grounds in February 1965. Consequently, the RAF also acquired a similar F4 Phantom as an air defence aircraft and equipped it with a reconnaissance pod that fulfilled one role previously envisaged for TSR2. The RAF was allowed to order a subsonic upgrade of Kestrel to replace ground-attack Hunters as a result of the P.1154 cancellation, which in turn became the Harrier.

The one major question that will never be answered is: would PCB and the BS.100 engine actually have worked? Though a PCB system was ground run attached to a Pegasus, it was never fitted and run on any of the few BS.100 engines built.

Hot gas ingestion was the biggest problem that would have had to be overcome, especially on take-off or coming into the hover, while another would have been foreign object damage from anything in the path of around 35,000lb of thrust. Other issues that needed consideration were said to include melted runway tarmac and potentially even melted carrier deck plates.

In the end, government finances put an end to what could have been a capable and possibly lucrative aircraft, certainly there was more chance of P.1154 meeting the operational specification set for it when compared to TSR2. The true operational potential of V/STOL would become clearer within 18 months

Left: Usually hidden by the front nozzle, it's easy to see that the main centre section of the Pegasus engine is effectively a self-contained unit. This allows a significant percentage of the intake air to be diverted to the front nozzles and the remainder enters the central high-pressure stages in a conventional manner, exiting via the rear nozzles.

Below: Newark Air Museum's BS.53 Pegasus. Compared to the BS.100 the original BS.53 engine is slightly smaller in diameter and not that much shorter, yet somehow looks much smaller.

of the cancellation, after completion of trials with the tripartite Kestrel squadron. A great deal of the equipment that was planned and already under development for P.1154 benefited the Harrier programme in terms of avionic systems, but both the RAF and Royal Navy could have had a supersonic V/STOL aircraft 50 years before the arrival of the F-35.

A wooden mock-up of the P.1154 at Hawker's Kingston factory. (Alamy stock images)

P.1154's rival, the Dassault Mirage IIIV, mounting eight Rolls-Royce RB.162 for lift only, plus a P&W/SNECMA TF104 for forward thrust.

A manufacturers model of HS681 at RAF Museum Midlands. On paper it had short take-off performance on par with the American YC-14 and YC-15 STOL transport demonstrators that flew 10 years later.

Cancelled on the same day as P.1154, the Hawker Siddeley HS.681 V/STOL transport was potentially another host for the vectored thrust Pegasus, though the Rolls-Royce Medway and lift engines were also being considered. Either would have given enviable STOL capability while retaining transit speeds well above those of turboprop equivalents. The final decision on engine choice was never made by the government before cancellation, with a great deal of behind-the-scenes lobbying from Bristol-Siddeley for the BS.100 and Rolls-Royce with the Medway, combined with podded banks of RB.162 or RB.175 lift engines.

Envisaged as supporting P.1154 field operations, the strategic changes brought on by the politics involved with the 'withdrawal from east of Suez' meant the need for an aircraft such as HS.681 reduced dramatically, and the prospect of cancellation for this and the other contenders vying for the same contract had been expected for some time.

Hawker P.1127

The P.1127 resulted from a meeting of minds between two of the giants of British aviation, Sir Sydney Camm at Hawker and Dr Stanley Hooker at Bristol Siddeley. The idea of a vectored thrust-powered aircraft actually originated in France with designer Michel Wibault, who drew plans for a single-seat attack aircraft that was propelled by centrifugal blowers linked to fuselage side-mounted controllable nozzles. By 1956, these designs had attracted the attention of the NATO Mutual Weapons Development Program (MWDP) in Paris. Around the same time, the Fiat G-91 light strike fighter had just flown, after being selected as the winner of NATO's NBMR-1 competition for a light fighter. The Fiat was powered by Bristol Siddeley's Orpheus jet engine, and its probable that details of Wibault's 'Gyroptere' were seen by Dr Hooker possibly during discussions at NATO over the G-91. They were then discussed with his team at Bristol, specifically with a young engineer called Gordon Lewis.

Having dismissed Wibault's centrifugal fan idea as inefficient and heavy, discussions between Bristol and Michel Wibault eventually resulted in patents being granted to both Wibault and Gordon Lewis for a new engine derived from the Orpheus, with an additional large low-pressure compressor section using fans from the Olympus engine, with power delivered initially via a pair but ultimately by four rotating nozzles. This was christened the BS.53 Pegasus. With the MWDP funding 75 per cent of the development, and the remaining 25 per cent being company-funded. Bristol now needed an airframe to match the engine, and a brochure was despatched to Hawker, where Sydney Camm's project engineer Ralph Hooper quickly designed an aircraft around the new engine – the P.1127.

Although he saw P.1127 fly and his ideas of a vectored thrust-powered aircraft realised, Michel Wibault died in 1963, aged 66.

A stroke of genius within the Pegasus design originated not with the engine manufacturer at Bristol, but from Ralph Hooper at Hawker. For an aircraft intended to hover, it needed as few physical turning forces acting upon it as possible. In a conventional engine, all the shafts and fan blades usually rotate in the same direction. This creates centrifugal forces that act upon the aircraft, which if you could suspend the aircraft along its centre axis, would induce it to roll. In Pegasus, the low-pressure turbine blades rotate counter to the high-pressure stages, equalising the turning forces and removing the induced roll. Without the need to compensate for engine-derived rotational force, the control effects of the 'puffer ducts' first seen on Rolls-Royce's TMR and Shorts SC.1 and incorporated on P.1127 were maximi d, while the demands on the auto-stabilisation system were reduced.

The first P.1127, XP831 now hangs in the Science Museum in London. On the floor below is an excellent Pegasus display with lighting to show the hot and cold nozzles.

Various iterations of the original P.1127 airframe design eventually resulted in the characteristic shape that was carried through the Harrier family. High wings and tail to clear the jet efflux from the side-mounted nozzles, both with a distinct dihedral, a nose wheel and central undercarriage unit quite close together to support the main loads, with wing-tip outriggers to keep the aircraft upright.

The first prototype, XP831, began tethered hovering flights on 21 October 1960, and over the next five months, further hovering flights with high-speed taxiing eventually led to a first flight from a conventional take-off on 13 March 1961. By July of the same year, a second prototype, XP836, joined the project, allowing Hawker's test pilots Bill Bedford and Hugh Merryweather to expand the flight envelope. By 12 September 1961, both pilots had achieved full translational flights, from the hover to forward flight and vice versa despite the loss of XP836 (one of the forward cold engine nozzles, which at the time were fibreglass, detached following a high-speed run, forcing Bill Bedford to eject). But by then, sufficient faith was seen in the vectored thrust concept that a second development batch of P.1127s was ordered. The fibreglass nozzles would be replaced with a lightweight steel version.

The value of the information gathered from flying these aircraft, which fed into a number of other projects as well as Kestrel and Harrier cannot be underestimated and the P.1127s continued to be flown for research purposes until the mid-1970s.

Close ups of the jet nozzles on the P.1127, this photo shows the port wing tip unit housed in the forward section of the outrigger undercarriage fairing.

Brooklands Museum's Hawker P.1127, XP984, perched over the edge of the mezzanine floor above the 'factory' area. This was the final airframe built and incorporated sweep to rear of the wing, which carried over on to the Kestrel and the Harrier. Note the nose hover control opening. (Courtesy Brooklands Museum)

The tail extension houses three nozzles, port, starboard and ventral.

P.1227 XP836 in flight; the original slightly swept air intakes noticeable.

Right: **A flight of four Kestrel FGA.1s from the Tripartite evaluation squadron.**

Below: **XS695, Kestrel FGA.1. Restored at the Michael Beetham Conservation Centre at RAF Museum Midlands during the mid 2010s, and now on display in the Test Flight hangar.**

Hawker Kestrel

As ever, funding for P.1127 and Pegasus development had been problematic from the start, with funds coming from NATO, the USA and West Germany, but financial backing from the UK government had been lacking. By early 1962, Hawker believed that the RAF saw no operational use for P.1127 in its current guise; it also suspected that if a V/STOL aircraft was purchased, the RAF favoured the French supersonic Mirage IIIV, rather than the proposed British P.1154.

However, after several meetings between representatives from the USA, West Germany and the UK, an agreement was finally reached in January 1963 for a batch of nine definitive P.1127s. These were christened Kestrel and built with every advance gained from the P.1127 programme to date. These improvements included the final wing shape, fitted to the last P.1127 built, XP984, the most powerful Pegasus 5 engine, which by now was generating 18,000lb of thrust, allowing a fuel plus weapon load of 2,200lb from a vertical take-off, or 6,500lb from a short rolling take-off. The new, slightly shorter wings included a hard point for a rocket pod or external fuel tank but crucially, the whole airframe was to be stressed for combat flying. The first Kestrel taxied out at Hawker's Dunsfold factory on 5 March 1964, becoming airborne two days later, piloted by Alfred William 'Bill' Bedford.

By July 1965, and with P.1154 cancelled three months earlier, an agreement was reached between the UK, USA and West Germany [6] to create a dedicated evaluation squadron with a wide-ranging remit to determine the suitability and practicalities of operating V/STOL strike and reconnaissance aircraft from both a conventional runway environment and unprepared areas in the field. Further discussions led to this unit being located at RAF West Raynham in Norfolk.

Nine Kestrels were delivered to the tri-partite evaluation unit, although XS696 played little part in the proceedings, after an unfortunate accident when a US pilot failed to release the parking brake during take-off, causing it to swing off the runway and leading to it being written off.

The Kestrel and the evaluation squadron created to explore its potential was an outstanding success, completing more than 600 hours of intense flying over 938 operational sorties, with no further losses. The Kestrels often flew from unprepared sites, resulting in jet exhausts causing ground erosion with consequent potential for foreign object ingestion in the engine. Many lessons learned here were later adopted and expanded by the fledgling RAF Harrier force.

Finally disbanded on 28 February 1966, six of the aircraft departing for the USA to work with NASA and elsewhere, while XS963 and XS965 remained in the UK as part of the Harrier development programme.

Of the two UK-bound aircraft, XS963 crashed at Boscombe Down following engine problems in September 1967, Sqn Ldr Hugh Rigg successfully ejecting. XS965, which is now at the RAF Museum Midlands, was lucky to survive after being written off following a landing short of the Boscombe Down runway in March 1967. Repaired by the Royal Navy Engineering College in 1973, utilising the wing unit from previously mentioned crash victim XS696, it went to Royal Naval Air Station (RNAS) Culdrose as an instructional airframe, before arriving at its current home at RAF Museum Midlands.

One further Kestrel, XS694, has now returned to UK shores, to the Wings Museum in West Sussex. Originally shipped to the USA and assigned to Eglin Air Force Base in Florida, it was later transferred to NASA's Langley Research Center, at Langley Field, Virginia. After suffering extensive damage in a crash during 1967, it was stripped for spares and spent much of its life as an attraction at a paintball range.

The first true production version of the P.1127 family arrived in RAF service in the shape of Harrier GR.1 XV747 upon delivery to 233 Operational Conversion Unit (OCU) at RAF Wittering on 1 April

---

6   West German interest was primarily technical and following involvement in Kestrel, went on to build the V/STOL development aircraft, mentioned earlier, hence the common sight of tripartite markings on P.1127s

Above and below: Harrier GR.1, XV741, which despite its fame as a race winner, was later converted to GR.3 spec with the laser nose and served with 233 Operational Conversion Unit (OCU). It was converted back to GR.1/air race spec by JetArt Aviation. (Courtesy Brooklands Museum)

1969, with No 1 Squadron the first front-line unit, formed later the same month (XV747 was later converted to GR.3 standard but crashed in November 1987).

The capabilities of Britain's new 'Jump Jet' eventually appeared on British tea-time television news screens when it won the *Daily Mail* Trans-Atlantic Air Race in 1969. Taking off from 'RAF St Pancras', which was the old coal yard at St Pancras railway station in London and landing at Bristol Basin, New York, it arrived in a time of 6 hours and 11 minutes, aided by ferry tanks and the assistance of Victor

Kestrel XS694 as it arrived from the USA. The main fuselage has survived reasonably well. (Courtesy Wings Aviation Museum)

Former 233 OCU Harrier GR3, XV748, looking very clean and shiny. (Courtesy Yorkshire Air Museum)

tankers throughout the flight. Also fitted for the race and very rarely used in more usual circumstances, were ferry-tip extensions, fitted in place of the standard combat wing tip, beyond the outrigger wheels and control ducts. These improved lift and range, at the expense of manoeuvrability.

With unique flight characteristics, the P.1127 family was never going to be an easy aircraft to pilot, so a two-seat trainer had been envisaged since its inception. The first prototype Harrier T.2 XW174 eventually appeared on 29 April 1969, though an engine failure cut short its career less than two months later, forcing pilot Duncan Simpson to eject. Second prototype XW175 was delivered in July 1969 and by the time the first two-seaters were released to the OCU, they had gained more powerful Pegasus Mk102 engines and had been designated T.2A.

The GR.3 was the last of the original all-metal, wholly Hawker-designed-and-built RAF Harrier family, replacing the pointed nose of the GR.1 with a dolphin-shaped nose that housed a Laser Rangefinder and Marked Target Seeker (LRMTS).

Unofficially, but technically, there is an additional Harrier subversion, the GR.3C, C for Corporate, after the operation to liberate the Falklands. RAF Wittering's engineering personnel, alongside specialists from manufacturers, spent long days and nights rushing modifications into place ready for aircraft deployment to the Falklands' Task Force. This included wiring to allow fitment of Sidewinder missiles on the outboard pylons, a modified starboard Aden gun pod with the hastily constructed 'Blue Eric' ECM unit inside. This latter item utilised parts borrowed from the Sky Shadow pod that was used on Panavia Tornado. The countermeasures system was completed with a Tracor AN/ALE-40 chaff and flare dispenser, fitted in a panel that replaced the normal access hatch to the rear electronics bay, just behind the air brake. Early ad hoc trials dispensing chaff bundles simply stashed behind the air brake and released with a blip of the air brake when needed were less than successful, casting a cloud of chaff over Wittering's runway and obliterating the airfield on radar for three days until it dispersed.

The final and most advanced marks of the original P.1127/Kestrel/Harrier family belonged to the Royal Navy with the Sea Harrier. Eager to retain some sort of fixed-wing combat aircraft once the demise of its conventional aircraft carriers had been confirmed, the Admiralty had managed to procure what were originally called 'through deck cruisers'. At first, these seemed a little large solely as anti-submarine helicopter platforms, but the arrival of the Sea Harrier gave them far greater capability, which was further enhanced by the fitment of a ski-jump to the end of the deck that allowed higher take-off weights following a rolling take-off.

Ground crew work on one of the ten RAF 1 Squadron Harriers modified to GR.3C standard and deployed to the Falklands in 1982. Paveway II laser-guided bombs on the outer pylons were reliant upon targets being illuminated by a ground-based designator. (Getty Images)

Somewhere in Germany? Norway? Denmark? RAF Harrier GR3 in what became its natural habitat.

A pair of Sea Harrier FRS.1 come in to land. Combat proven in the Falklands, greatly aided by using AIM-9L Sidewinder all-aspect AAMs. Compared to the RAF's GR.3, the short pointed nose houses a Ferranti Blue Fox air intercept radar, while the raised cockpit with a bubble canopy improves all-round visibility. (Alamy stock images)

Newark's *Shar 2*, ZA176. Note the greatly changed nose profile between the original Blue Fox-equipped Sea Harrier in the previous photo and the Blue Vixen equipped of FA.2.

Entering service in 1979, the major outward change to the RAF Harrier was the new nose to accommodate the Ferranti Blue Fox radar, the ability to launch AIM-9 Sidewinder air-to-air missiles, plus changes in the metals used for some components to make them less susceptible to sea water corrosion.

The entry of the Sea Harrier into service was timely. Only three years later, in April 1982, all the Sea Harrier aircraft that the Royal Navy could muster, along with ten RAF Harriers crammed aboard HMS *Invincible* and *Hermes* filled news broadcasts on a nightly basis as part of Operation *Corporate* to return British sovereignty to the Falkland Islands. Greatly aided by the supply of AIM-9L all aspect Sidewinder missiles from the US, the navy Sea Harriers took a heavy toll of Argentine aircraft at no loss to themselves in air-to-air combat.

Lessons learnt in the Falklands were incorporated into the development of the final 'old school' Harrier design, the Sea Harrier FA.2, the prototype of which appeared in 1988. The FA/2 was equipped with a much more powerful Ferranti Blue Vixen radar, which allowed carriage of AIM-120 AMRAAM air-to-air missiles and provided beyond visual range target engagement for the first time, Sea Eagle anti-shipping missiles and even WE.177A tactical nuclear bombs. This amounted to a huge increase in all-round capability and the Shar 2, as they were usually called, saw the Navy's Harrier fleet to the end in 2006.

The Indian Navy also procured the original version of the Sea Harrier in 1979, and 30 eventually arrived in service from 1983, replacing the 1950s vintage Hawker Sea Hawk. Foregoing the same radar and missile upgrades adopted by the Royal Navy for the FA2 due to political restrictions, India instead purchased Israeli Elta radars and Rafael 'Derby' medium-range air-to-air range missiles. The Indian Navy phased out its Sea Harriers in 2012.

Chapter 9

Blackburn
NA.39 – Buccaneer

Naval Staff Requirement NA.39 (later M.148T) was issued in July 1953 for a long-range, low-level, carrier-based strike aircraft, capable of 550kn at 200ft, with a combat radius of 400 miles and able to deliver nuclear or conventional weapons against Soviet harbours and ships, but especially the latest 'Sverdlov' class of cruisers, which the Royal Navy considered a major threat.

Several companies submitted designs for the requirement, and Armstrong Whitworth's AW.168, Short Brother's PD.13 and Blackburn's NA.39 were chosen for further evaluation. The AW.168 resembled the French Sud-Ouest Vautour, with under-wing engine pods that also housed the undercarriage and similar DH Gyron Juniors to those fitted to the Buccaneer S.1. The design also incorporated an internal bomb bay. Short's PD.13 looked far more advanced, with side-mounted RR Avon RA.19 engines, but with highly swept wings that were a version of the 'aero-isoclinic' design seen on the Shorts SB.4, in which the outer fifth of the wings also act as elevator and aileron; the PD.13 was also designed to be supersonic. However, Short couldn't deliver within the Navy's desired timeframe, and the wing design was considered something of a risk. The AW.168 was less advanced than the other two contenders and had little development potential, resulting in Blackburn's offering being accepted for production. The design adopted an area-ruled fuselage to reduce high-speed drag with a two-person cockpit arranged in tandem; a one piece, milled forged steel main spar to increase strength; the wings incorporated boundary layer control using engine bleed air on both leading and trailing edges as well as on the all-moving tailplane, doubling the available lift from what was a relatively small wing, especially at low speeds, which greatly reduced the take-off and landing speeds. One unique feature was a revolving bomb bay door, which allowed a zero-drag internal weapons carriage.

The first prototype, XK486, flew on the 30 April 1958, though this was lost in a crash in 1960. Two more prototypes were also lost during development, both along with their aircrew, the last while undergoing carrier trials in 1961.

The NA.39 was christened 'Buccaneer' and began its operational career in 1962, though it didn't take long to recognise the shortcomings of the lack of power from the two Gyron Junior engines. This was especially pronounced in hot climates, to such an extent that the Buccaneer could not perform a fully loaded take-off. This forced the Royal Navy to retain a number of Supermarine Scimitars, which the Buccaneer was supposed to replace, for use as tanker aircraft, allowing a fully armed but under-fuelled aircraft to immediately tank up with a circling Scimitar once airborne. Plans for a permanent solution were already underway, with new engines the only option, and the Rolls-Royce Spey was eventually chosen. This necessitated a redesign of the air intakes to allow increased airflow for the turbofan Spey, as well as internal changes to the engine housing clamps, though adoption of this engine also gave the aircraft a marked increase in range due to much better fuel consumption, as well as greater reliability. The opportunity was also taken to change many other systems for newer, improved designs during the engine change process, and the new version became the Buccaneer S.2.

Housed in Cobham Hall at the FAA Museum, RNAS Yeovilton, XK488 is the third prototype built and the only surviving NA.39.

Another view of the NA.39 at Cobham Hall. The metal 'debris' surrounding it are parts from assorted Fairey Barracudas that the museum is rebuilding into one aircraft.

Blackburn proposed the Buccaneer to meet Air Ministry requirements for the RAF on at least two occasions both during and after TSR2 had been cancelled. All proposals were rejected, with some commentators suggesting the reason was mainly because they were derived from a naval aircraft. Blackburn didn't really push hard enough for either to be considered. One of the proposals, made when TSR2 was still a live project but the clouds of doubt about its future were already gathering, was P.150, a supersonic version with a lengthened fuselage, longer wings, and reheated Spey engines. This may well have given the RAF an aircraft close to the original GOR.339 specification, but the RAF was adamant it wanted TSR2. Following the eventual cancellation of TSR.2, further political meddling and the on/off decision to acquire F-111, the RAF was forced to relent and adopt the standard S.2 in 1969 to cover the attack roles planned for TSR.2. The RAF incorporated all the Navy's remaining S.2s in 1979 following the decommissioning of the only remaining conventional aircraft carrier, HMS Ark Royal.

Finally, and for the next 25 years, the RAF had a superlative low-level strike aircraft, excelling on the ranges at *Red Flag* in the USA, often to the stunned amazement of the range controllers when they appeared overhead, usually undetected.

The Buccaneer also unexpectedly went to war in the Gulf in 1990, when it was realised the Pave Spike laser-targeting pod fitted to the Tornado wouldn't work, because the Tornado wasn't steady enough in flight to keep the laser on target, yet it worked fine on the old Buccaneer. Hastily prepared by the engineering teams at RAF Lossiemouth, who incorporated the Pave Spike pods, AN/ALQ 101 ECM pods, fitment for AIM-9 Sidewinder and the same AN-ALE40 chaff and flare dispenser urgently fitted to the Harrier GR.3 for the Falklands conflict. Eventually, 12 aircraft would participate, in their tasteful 'Desert Pink' paint scheme, flying more than 200 missions and illuminating targets for around 170 Paveway laser-guided bombs that were dropped from Tornados, alongside 48 from the Buccaneers and with no

Above left: **Buccaneer S1 at Newark.**

Above right: **S2 on the flight deck at Yeovilton. Compare the size of the S1 air intakes, with those of the S2, the latter needing a greatly increased intake diameter for the Rolls-Royce Spey, which replaced the Gyron Junior of the S1.**

aircraft losses. The usual aircraft formation was of two Buccaneers with a Pave Spike pod on each, thus allowing one pod to fail, alongside a four-ship Tornado formation.

Despite the aircraft's reputation for robustness and the inherent strength of the steel main spars, the fatigue life had been calculated using the original wing profile. Modifications to produce the S.2 had included a slight increase in wing area to reduce drag caused by the new enlarged engine nacelles, and unexpectedly this had reduced the anticipated fatigue life in the front spar. Following a fatal crash involving XV345 while on *Red Flag* exercises in the USA, a fleet-wide investigation revealed cracks in the front spar on a number of aircraft. Many never flew again, while others were re-sparred by BAe or had smaller cracks repaired.

Eventually bowing out in March 1994, the Buccaneer finished service in its originally intended role as a maritime strike aircraft, albeit land based, but still able to carry double the number of Sea Eagle missiles than the Tornado that replaced it.

Above: The Buccaneer incorporated quite a large and highly effective airbrake, formed by splitting the tail cone.

Right: The rotating bomb bay door was never replicated on any other British aircraft. Later marks had a bulged door containing additional fuel.

Newark's S1 in the extra dark sea grey over anti-flash white scheme used by the Fleet Air Arm during the 1960s.

Operation *Granby* trio: a 'Pave Spike'-equipped Buccaneer alongside a 55 Squadron Victor K2 and 'Paveway'-armed Tornado. (Crown copyright)

Buccaneer S2B XX901 in *Desert Storm* camouflage. (Courtesy Yorkshire Air Museum)

Visiting

Aircraft	Serial	Museum	Notes	Website
		Aerospace Bristol		aerospacebristol.org
Bristol Britannia	G-ALRX		Cockpit section	
		Avro Heritage Centre, Woodford		www.avroheritagemuseum.co.uk
Avro 707C	WZ744			
		Boscombe Down Aviation Collection		www .boscombedownaviationcollection .co.uk
Avro 707A	WZ736			
		Brooklands Museum, Surrey		www.brooklandsmuseum.com
Hawker P.1127	XP981			
Hawker Harrier GR.1	XV741			
		FAA Museum, RNAS Yeovilton		www.nmrn.org.uk/visit-us /fleet-air-arm-museum
BS100 - Engine				
Blackburn NA.39	XK488		Cobham Hall store	
Hawker P.1052	VX272		Cobham Hall store	
Hawker P.1127	XP980			
Scimtar F.1	XD317			
		IWM Duxford		www.iwm.org.uk/visits /iwm-duxford
Harrier GR.3	XZ133			
Viscount	G-ALWF			
		Midland Air Museum		www.midlandairmuseum.co.uk
Blue Steel			Missile	
Boulton Paul P.111A	VT935			
Hunter F.6A	XF382			
		Newark Air Museum		www.newarkairmuseum.org
Reid and Sigrist SR.4 Bobsleigh	VZ728		G-AGOS	

Aircraft	Serial	Museum	Notes	Website
Meteor FR.9 MOD	VZ607		VTOL Testbed	
			Engine	
DH.114 Heron	G-ANXB			
Blue Steel and Stentor Rocket Engine			Missile	
Bloodhound and Radar Unit			Missile	
Hunter T7	XL618			
Hunter F1	WT651			
Harrier FA.2	ZA146			
Buccaneer S.1	XN964			
Avro Ashton II	WB491			
BS.53 Pegasus			Engine	
		Norfolk and Suffolk Aviation Museum		www.aviationmuseum.net
Hunter FGA9	XG254			
Bloodhound Mk1 & Radar Unit			Missile	
Javelin FAW9	XH892			
BS.53 Pegasus			Engine	
		RAF Museum Midlands		www.rafmuseum.org.uk
Prone Meteor F8	WK935			
Hawker Kestrel	XS695			
Blue Steel			Missile	
Douglas Skybolt			Missile	
Yellow Sun, Red Beard			Bombs	
Bloodhound WE.177			Missile	
Hawker P.1121		Incomplete fuselage	Not on public display	
		RAAF Museum, Point Cook, Victoria, Australia		www.airforce.gov.au/raaf-museum
Avro 707A	WD280			
		Science Museum, London		www.sciencemuseum.org.uk
Hawker P.1127	XP831			
Shorts SC.1	XG900			
	XJ314			

Aircraft	Serial	Museum	Notes	Website
		Ulster Folk and Transport Museum, Northern Ireland		www.nmni.com/our-museums /Ulster-Transport-Museum/Home
Shorts SC.1	XG905			
		Yorkshire Air Museum, Elvington		yorkshireairmuseum.org
Buccaneer S2B	XX901			
Harrier GR3	XV748			
Victor K2	XL231			
Nimrod MR2	XV250			

Supermarine Scimitar F1, XD317 at the RNAS Museum, Yeovilton. Retained as a tanker aircraft for the S.1 Buccaneers, the refuelling pod can just be seen under the port wing. The only remnant of a prototype Scimitar is the cockpit section of WT859 at the Boscombe Down Aviation Collection at Old Sarum.

Bibliography

Project Cancelled, Derek Wood, McDonald and James, 1975

British Secret Projects: Jet Bombers Since 1949, Tony Butler, Midland Publishing, 2003

British Secret Projects 1: Jet Fighters Since 1950, Tony Butler, Crecy Publishing, 2017

Cold War Interceptor, Dan Sharp, Morton's Media Group, 2019

Hawker P.1103 and P.1121 – Camm's Last Fighter Projects, Paul Martell-Mead and Barrie, Hygate, Blue Envoy Press, 2015

Hawker P.1127, Hawker Siddeley Kestrel and Harrier Mk1–4, Tony Butler, Hall Park

Hawker's Early Jets, Christopher Budgen, Air World, 2022

TSR2 – Britain's Lost Bomber, Damian Burke, Crowood Aviation, 2010

Aeroplane Monthly, Key Publishing

British X-Planes – The Jet Era, Aviation Archive

Skybolt, Nicholas Hill, Fonthill Media, 2019

Britain and the Bomb, W.J. Nutall, Whittles Publishing, 2019

Pegasus – The Heart of the Harrier, Andrew Dow, Pen & Sword, 2009

Flying The Buccaneer: Britain's Cold War Warrior, Peter Caygill, Pen & Sword, 2008

British Airliner Prototypes Since 1945, Stephen Skinner, Midland Publishing, 2008

From Lysander to Lightning: Teddy Petter, Aircraft Designer, Glyn Davies, The History Press, 2014

The Secret World of Vickers Guided Weapons, John Forbat, The History Press, 2009

Swift Justice – The Full Story of the Supermarine Swift, Nigel Walpole, Pen & Sword, 2004

Nimrod: Rise and Fall, Tony Blackman, Grub Street Publishing, 2013

Comet! The World's First Jet Airliner, Graham M. Simons, Pen & Sword, 2013

Nimrod: Rise and Fall, Tony Blackman, Grub Street Publishing, 2013

Blue Streak: Britain's Medium Range Ballistic Missile, John Boyes, Fonthill Media, 2019

Other books you might like:

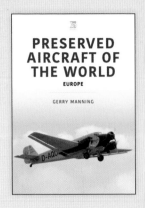

For our full range of titles please visit:

shop.keypublishing.com/books